# Contents

**The Bible Reading Fellowship**
15 The Chambers, Vineyard
Abingdon OX14 3FE
**brf.org.uk**

BRF is a Registered Charity (233280)

ISBN 978 0 85746 453 8
First published 2017
10 9 8 7 6 5 4 3 2 1 0


**Acknowledgements**
Scripture quotations taken from The Holy Bible, New International Version (Anglicised edition) copyright © 1973, 1978, 1984, 2011 by Biblica, are used by permission of Hodder & Stoughton Publishers, an Hachette UK company. All rights reserved. 'NIV' is a registered trade mark of Biblica (formerly International Bible Society). UK trademark number 1448790.

Scripture quotations taken from The Holy Bible, New International Version, copyright © 1973, 1978, 1984, 1995 by International Bible Society, are used by permission of Hodder & Stoughton, a member of the Hachette Livre UK Group. All rights reserved. 'NIV' is a registered trademark of International Bible Society. UK trademark number 1448790.

Scripture quotations taken from The New Revised Standard Version of the Bible, Anglicised Edition, copyright © 1989, 1995 by the Division of Christian Education of the National Council of the Churches of Christ in the USA, are used by permission. All rights reserved.

Extracts from the Authorised Version of the Bible (The King James Bible), the rights in which are vested in the Crown, are reproduced by permission of the Crown's Patentee, Cambridge University Press.

Extract from *As a Child* by Phil Steer, published by lulu.com, 2012

Every effort has been made to trace and contact copyright owners for material used in this resource. We apologise for any inadvertent omissions or errors, and would ask those concerned to contact us so that full acknowledgement can be made in the future.

A catalogue record for this book is available from the British Library

Printed by Gutenberg Press, Tarxien, Malta

# The Editor writes...

Welcome to *Quiet Spaces*.

We are journeying through Lent with Matthew this year, which will give the opportunity for an overview of the whole of Jesus' life up to Easter.

Lent can be a good time for considering our spiritual life and an opportunity to try new things and set ourselves new challenges. This Lent you might like to consider how you prepare for your prayer times. Do you suddenly stop the busyness of life and expect instantly to be still and quiet with God, or do you choose a time when you have slowed down first and so come without a mind and heart full of the day? We don't all have the luxury of taking time to prepare, but we can all take a few moments as we start. Sometimes I find music helps, playing a quiet piece and allowing it to wash over me as I let go of all I've brought with me. Or sometimes I recall the things that are on my mind and likely to distract me, and I offer them to God, asking him to keep them and look after them while I spend time with him. He may put them carefully on a shelf or place them gently in a special box. At the end of the sessions I take back what he has been saving, often leaving one or two things for his longer-term keeping. Psalms or other favourite Bible passages are another good way into prayer, either allowing a whole psalm to wash over me, or reading until one phrase leads me to God, and then staying with that phrase.

Other times I sit and pause, waiting for life to settle and for me to see God in the midst of it, either in a special chair, or looking at a special view; remembering when I have met with God there before and acknowledging his faithfulness to me.

Then, as you settle, ask God to help you be still and able to recognise his presence with you.

Have a good Lent and a joyful Easter.

*Sally Smith*

# Writers in this issue

**Sue McCoulough** worked for a number of years at the BBC. She was then prayer coordinator at Tearfund. Now a volunteer for the church alliance Restored, which seeks to combat domestic violence against women, Sue enjoys walking, creative writing and leading Quiet Days.

**Andrea Skevington** lives in Suffolk with her family. She writes for both adults and children, winning the Christian Book of the Year award (Speaking Volumes) for her retelling, *The Lion Classic Bible* (Lion Hudson, 2011). She also enjoys storytelling for children and running creative writing seminars for adults.

**Janet Fletcher** is Associate Vicar in the Bro Ystumanner Ministry Area, and Diocesan Spirituality Officer in Bangor Diocese, Church in Wales. She offers spiritual direction, and enjoys leading Quiet Days and retreats, and teaching and writing on prayer and spirituality.

**Sally Smith** enjoys creating spaces that enable encounters with God through leading Quiet Days and creating prayer corners and stations. She has led prayer groups in her local church, works as a spiritual director and writes and produces education materials.

**Helen Julian CSF** is an Anglican Franciscan sister and a priest, currently serving her community as Minister General. She has written three books for BRF and contributes to BRF's *New Daylight* Bible reading notes.

**Lisa Cherrett** is BRF's Project Editor and Managing Editor for Bible reading notes. She sings, writes haiku poetry and is interested in the relationship between Christianity and contemporary culture. She blogs at lisannie44.wordpress.com.

**Sally Welch** is Vicar of Charlbury and Area Dean of Chipping Norton. Sally also leads training events for the Diocese of Oxford in the area of spirituality and is a Diocesan Labyrinth Coordinator. She has written a number of books and is also the editor of BRF's *New Daylight* Bible reading notes.

**Jean Marie Dwyer OP** is a Dominican nun of the Queen of Peace Monastery, Squamish, British Columbia, Canada. The monastery is dedicated to silence, prayer, study and intercession for all people. She is the author of *The Sacred Place of Prayer* (BRF, 2013) and *The Unfolding Journey: The God Within: Etty Hillesum and Meister Eckhart* (Novalis, 2014).

**Lynne Chitty** was Deacon at Gloucester Cathedral and now lives in a caravan in the grounds of Mill House Retreats in Devon. She combines leading creative writing courses with times of solitude and has a variety of rescue animals.

# Three things remain: faith, hope and love

*Sue McCoulough*

## Three things remain

### Introduction

As a church choir member, I often sing at weddings. If I had a pound for every time the bride and groom pick 1 Corinthians 13 as a reading, I'd be pretty rich! Yet it's obvious why many couples feature it in their big day. This section of Paul's letter is both poetically beautiful and full of joyful wisdom, summarising what's important to lasting relationships.

In 1 Corinthians 1—12, which you could read if you have time, Paul offers solutions to division and disorder within the Church. Chapters 1—6 focus on these issues. He goes on to warn against conforming to worldly values (7) and idolatry (8 and 10). Believers are challenged to accept human weaknesses (9:19–23) and natural diversity as part of the united 'body' of the Church (11—12). Christians are encouraged to examine themselves, recommit to the values of Jesus, then 'model' him.

There is a danger, though, of modelling Christ in a head-centred way, as we can end up creating a tick list of achievements or failures. Instead, we're urged to engage with the Spirit, who transforms individual believers and churches holistically.

Take a piece of modelling dough or clay. Alternatively, use a large piece of paper and pencil. Shape or draw a simple outline of a human being: think of it as yourself. Now, looking at your creation without judgement, ask yourself the following. Are there:

- any distinctive characteristics?
- any lumps or bumps speaking of problems for 'the body'?
- any things you'd like to add, accentuate or remove?

Jot down what you notice. Then, without trying to make sense of your figure's shape or prime characteristics, place it in the hands of God, the master potter. Imagine him taking loving hold of you. Watch as he holds, looks and begins to remodel.

If your figure feels misshapen, ask God how you might remould things. Wait patiently for a response before making any changes to your figure.

You could try the same exercise and produce a 'figure' that speaks of your church.

Finish with this prayer:

*Lord Jesus, I want to model you.*
*Help me focus on things that count eternally,*
*be faithful to your love,*
*hopeful, like treasure in clay jars, yet to be revealed.*
*And finally, vitally, help me abide in your love,*
*then grow in love for you and all creation. Amen*

## Faith and doubt

### Creative

Recently, a relation of mine read my writing and commented wistfully, 'I wish I could have faith.' But we all have faith in something, such as 'I believe in my children', 'I believe in my right to vote', even 'I don't believe in a God!'

Gerald Priestland spent years working in religious broadcasting but struggled with faith. He pointed out that 'trusting' and 'believing' are not the same thing, saying, 'I know that I trust; I hope I believe.' I sense he felt trust intuitively, while belief, for him, was something to be worked out or developed.

Christians often have the opposite problem: we may believe (in theory) but struggle (in practice) to trust that God's loving purposes will finally prevail.

Read John 20:24–29 thoughtfully. Notice how Thomas expresses doubt, then how Jesus handles Thomas' honest dilemma.

If you can, read other writings about 'Doubting Thomas'. A powerful poem is Malcolm Guite's 'St Thomas the Apostle' (on his website, and also available in print in *Sounding the Seasons: Seventy Sonnets for the Christian Year,* Canterbury Press, 2012). Guite praises Thomas for asking courageous questions when other disciples stay silent. He highlights the importance of human touch, arguing it can connect our wounded selves to a wounded God.

Find a picture of Christ on the cross, or appearing to the disciples after the resurrection. Now read through the Apostles' Creed as you look at the image of Christ. Are there any beliefs listed there that you struggle to affirm? If so, you might want to 'touch' Jesus in your picture.

Ask Jesus courageous questions, as Thomas did. Sense Christ's compassion flooding out to you. Let 'touching' his wounds heal your spirit, gradually helping you address any doubts.

## Touching faith

### Creative

Touching Jesus grew Thomas' faith; indeed, touch is a strong healing agent in the Gospels. As a doctor, Luke had special empathy with people considered 'untouchable'. He refers often to illnesses and afflictions, stressing that faith can cure them.

In Luke 8:40–48 we read of a woman who recognised that if she could just touch Jesus she would be healed.

*I didn't want to make a fuss. I suppose I should be used to it after twelve years. Doctors all saying they couldn't help. 'Women's problems,' they muttered, as if that made it all right. All my money was gone on failed treatments. My last resort was Jesus.*

*By the time I saw him, everyone was crowding in. I was being crushed out by people with bigger problems, shouting for help. I saw a rich man from the synagogue bend down, begging Jesus. 'Please save my daughter. She's dying!' What was my trouble compared to that?*

*Suddenly I was jolted forward from behind, to within an arm's length of Jesus! A little voice inside me begged, 'Just take a deep breath and inch nearer. Reach out, touch him. You'll be healed!'*

*With my arm outstretched, I stooped down, managing to reach the hem of his cloak. I held it for a moment between thumb and forefinger. Touching a thick, coarse weave of grey, ordinary material. Yet this touch sent a shiver down my spine.*

*Everything stopped. A moment's freeze-frame. Jesus stood still, shouting out, 'Who touched me?' One of the disciples said, 'Master, how should we know? The world and his wife are out today! You expect us to know who brushed against you?'*

*Terrified, I became rooted to the spot. Meanwhile, Jesus' eyes fixed on mine. Stumbling to my knees I cried out, 'Forgive me, master. I just knew you could heal me.'*

*How did those words come to me? Who told me I was healed? I just sensed it deep inside, so mumbled, 'Thank you, thank you.'*

*His smiled reply was brief but intense. 'Your faith has healed you. Go in peace.'*

*So I went and now I feel whole again.*

Notice the woman's humble, yet courageous faith. You don't have to be a woman to empathise with her plight. If you were in her shoes, would you seek Jesus' healing touch in a similar way?

Find a piece of cloth, preferably something rough and homespun, as Jesus would have worn. Take the cloth between thumb and forefinger and hold it as if holding Jesus' cloak. As you hold the cloak, try pouring out your heart to Jesus, without fear of what he, or others, might think. Don't worry if you can't put things into words. Aim to visualise touching him, then be aware of any response. Remember, Jesus wants you to both recognise and own up to your need. Stick your cloth to a larger piece of paper, perhaps the one containing your shape from the first exercise. Next to the cloth, write all the ways in which you want to touch Jesus. Offer these to him, slowly. Put the paper in front of you so that as you pray you can touch the cloth as the woman touched Jesus' cloak.

Finish by savouring Jesus' words 'Your faith has healed you. Go in peace.' Write these prominently on your paper. Gratefully absorb Jesus' promise.

## Emerging faith

### Going out

Jesus taught his disciples that after his death, his Father would send the Holy Spirit who would remain with them (John 14:15–31). Christians today still need awareness of the Spirit being in all times and places. This helps us lovingly proclaim Jesus in our attitudes, actions or words.

Read 1 Corinthians 13. Then go outside, into an area of noise, mess or disturbing upheaval. If you can't find one, go to a shop selling newspapers and study the headlines. If you're kept inside, find a picture, photograph or news story that seemingly challenges faith in God as ultimately having the last, loving say in our world.

Sit or stand for a while, noting anything that 'hits' your senses. If you react negatively, hand over any abhorrence or prejudice to God. Close your eyes. Inwardly say 'Love your neighbour', 'God's presence is with us' or any affirmation that helps you believe in Christ indwelling in all creation. Let the Spirit move you. Pray for God's understanding and compassion. If you are given any mental picture or literal symbol, hold on to it.

Move away from the area or picture. Has anything in your perspective changed? Perhaps you've glimpsed something attractive within the mess, or seen it through new eyes.

Thank God for any insights. Draw or write up your experiences. Is yours a 'bad news' story with potential for positive change? Ask God to help you share new faith in that area.

# Filled with hope

## Creative

In 1 Corinthians 13:13 Paul sandwiches hope between faith and love. Perhaps there's an analogy to be found between the qualities *faith*, *hope* and *love*, and the contents of a real sandwich.

Maybe faith can be likened to the base slice of bread on which hope and love are built up.

Hope is the in-between bit—the filling usually holding faith and love together. But, crucially, hope is often hidden from view by… a slice of love on top, definitely a gracious gift from God. This crowns faith and hope.

The writer of the letter to the Hebrews expands on this hidden aspect of hope in Hebrews 11. Faith is defined first as confidence in hopes about things yet unseen (vv. 1–2). Then he lists Old

Testament characters, living in a 'middle time' in Israel's history. They die before God's promises are fulfilled (v. 13). But even though God changes everything, at the right time, by sending his Son, Jesus, Christ's promises are yet to be seen fully worked out.

Why not make a 'hope' sandwich? As you butter the bread, remember the three parts of Paul's sandwich. As you choose your filling, think about your hopes and dreams for yourself, the world, perhaps family and friends. Has God given you a sign that 'things hoped for' will be fulfilled? Maybe disappointments or losses have dashed your hope of things holding together—the hope of 'a new heaven and a new earth' (Revelation 21:1).

As you place the three parts together, hold together the faith, hope and love you have experienced.

Before eating your hope sandwich, say this liturgy, inserting your longings in the gaps:

*How long, Lord, before your promises are fulfilled?*
*I lack understanding why…*
*I need patience to wait, to trust great things you've planned.*
*Help me believe you will fulfil…*

*I will savour memories—of things worked out in your time.*
*I relish your task—to build heaven on earth right now.*
*I will devour your promise—you will show me the next step.*
*I joyfully anticipate a time when … is overcome and when all the faithful can feast lovingly in your kingdom. Amen*

As you eat your sandwich, ask to be filled and satisfied with God's hope.

# Lord of all hopefulness

## Intercession

After a church day entitled 'A Certain Hope', I left with this saying:

> *God works in his way, whether we like it or not.*
> *God is here, whether we realise it or not.*
> *God has a wonderful plan, whether we know it or not.*
>
> Source unknown

Spend time praising God for 'being in charge'; there in our past, present and future, as promised in Psalm 139. Pray for people who are always there for you, or who exude hope even in difficult circumstances.

Or boldly offer God anything where feelings of hopelessness prevail, either in your own life or in someone else's. Add specific concerns about the world to your petitions. Don't be afraid to 'moan' to God; be honest about any desire for vengeance on others! Such lamentation can bridge a sense of powerlessness with new hopeful vision.

Finish by finding a copy of the popular hymn 'Lord of All Hopefulness'. If you can, sing a verse at a time, pausing to offer up the phases of the day to Jesus.

# Resurrection hope

## Reflective

> ***'I have told you these things, so that in me you may have peace. In this world you will have trouble. But take heart! I have overcome the world.'***
>
> JOHN 16:33

In my late teens, I rebelled against Jesus. Why? Because I didn't feel Jesus offered me the peace he promises to all disciples, as John mentions above. If anything, my non-Christian friends seemed more content and peaceful than me.

My reasoning to give up Christianity went something like this. What happened on the cross was intended to give me a guilt trip. If Jesus died for love of me, I was obliged to love him, even though I'd never seen him. What sort of love was that?

It didn't help that I was missing loved ones who had died: as non-believers, surely the Bible said I wouldn't see them again. What sort of hope was that?

My immature faith couldn't see beyond what happened on the cross. Later, I realised Jesus overcame sin with love at Calvary and beyond. I needed to stop making assumptions about how, when and where God's love and hopeful promises work.

Recall your past and present faith and experiences of resurrection hope. Now spend time meditating on one of the following passages:

- 1 Corinthians 15:13–57
- 2 Corinthians 4:13–16
- Romans 8:18–39

Do Paul's words help you think about death, and life beyond death, in a more hopeful way? If any loss is affecting you or someone you know at present, offer these struggles to Jesus. Whatever your 'feelings', take firm hold of his offer of peace. If you need an external focus, try gazing on a picture that offers hope beyond life as we know it today. Or listen to music that offers words of hope.

# Moved by hope

## Creative

A local television news item featured a large ballet school that was teaching movement to sufferers of Parkinson's disease. Their limited mobility was improving and once they were better able to express themselves, they also had greater hope.

Whatever your own physical capabilities, try some movement today to celebrate your earthly life. Think of different 'movements' you can make while praying to God, for example holding your arms together in front of your chest and then opening them out above your head (perhaps symbolising bringing God's kingdom into being).

Here are some hope-filled verses from the Bible that you could move to:

*... those who hope in the Lord will renew their strength. They will soar on wings like eagles; they will run and not grow weary, they will walk and not be faint.*
ISAIAH 40:31

*'I am with you always, to the very end of the age.'*
MATTHEW 28:20

*'For I know the plans I have for you,' declares the Lord, '... plans to give you hope and a future.'*
JEREMIAH 29:11

*May the God of hope fill you with all joy and peace as you trust in him, so that you may overflow with hope by the power of the Holy Spirit.*
ROMANS 15:13

*... Christ in you, the hope of glory.*
COLOSSIANS 1:27

# Letting God love

## Meditative

*Dear friends, let us love one another, for love comes from God. Everyone who loves has been born of God and knows God.*
1 JOHN 4:7

In the following verses, John claims that once we acknowledge Jesus as the Son of God, God lives in us and we in God (v. 15). We can be confident on the Day of Judgement because 'there is no fear in love' (v. 18).

Beautiful words. But maybe like me, you struggle to live them out. I like to think I love *most* people in the *agape* sense of the word. But then I find myself homing in on specific people I know, and all sorts of 'if only' thoughts come into my head. 'If only he were more tactful!' 'If only she didn't have that annoying laugh.' After bouts of such fault-finding, I wonder if I've ever really loved at all.

Each one of us has a slightly different struggle with the demands of love. But, at some point, most Christians ask, 'How can I possibly *begin* to love as God loves?'

Part of the answer comes in 1 John 4:19: we *can* love 'because he first loved us'. Then, as Paul reminds us in 1 Corinthians 13, God's love remains, whether we accept, ignore or even reject his love.

Try to acquire Edwina Gateley's poem, 'Let Your God Love You' (from her collection *In God's Womb: A Spiritual Memoir*, Orbis Books, 2009, and available online).

Now find a picture of Christ, perhaps as a baby in his mother's arms. Place it in front of you, lighting a candle nearby. Remember that we can only love God and others if we let the truth of God's unconditional love for us sink in first. If you can, read the poem slowly several times. If you don't have the poem, remain silently before the picture in the presence of Jesus.

Recognise any struggle you have to just 'be': silent and still before Love itself. Being active is easier for many people. If you find your mind wandering, be gentle with yourself. As the poem reminds us, he knows and understands. Sense God's enormous love flowing out to you as you continue to gaze at Jesus in the picture. Simply and quietly absorb all that he offers.

## Love in action

### Bible study

There's a story about a young child who lived next door to an elderly widower. The man wept and the little boy climbed onto his lap. The mother later asked the boy what he'd said to the neighbour. 'Nothing,' he replied. 'I just helped him cry.'

Sometimes we can express love better in actions, rather than words. Spend time now reflecting on the different ways Jesus demonstrated love. Pick one of the following passages. As you read it, recognise how Jesus shows love. Imagine being present in the scene and receiving that love direct from Jesus.

- The death and raising of Lazarus (John 11:1–44)
- Jesus washes the disciples' feet (John 13:1–17)
- Words from the cross (John 19:26–27; Luke 23:40–43)

What prompted Jesus' loving action? How did Jesus reveal love in that instance? What was the effect of his love on his witnesses? What was the effect of his love on you?

Thank Jesus for showing you love in action. Consider demonstrating love today, perhaps in a situation calling for 'tough love'. Remember to draw on Jesus' wisdom and loving strength before you act.

## Love has the last say

### Poetry

Paul ends 1 Corinthians 13 by proclaiming, 'And now these three remain: faith, hope and love. But the greatest of these is love.'

As you read the following, adapt it to match your own conclusions about love's ultimate power.

*When all's said and done,*
*Love counts.*
*Starts with Love that overcomes fear,*
*looks beyond self's clamouring for reward*
*by giving all.*
*This love comes to earth*
*embracing it till fit for eternity.*

*Can I match such love?*
*I've lost count of ways I've tried...*
*I've worked hard to serve others,*
*given my fair share of hugs or compliments,*
*even gritted my teeth and said nothing*
*when ignored or offended.*
*This love comes wearing a mask*
*to conceal a smug smile or fearful heart.*

*In time, the mask slips.*
*My anger and disappointment, exposed for all to see.*
*I cry out, 'I can't love!*
*All* ***my*** *love is*
*empty gesture, hideous noise, a clamouring for attention!'*

*Slowly, I reach out*
*to find cradling arms surround me.*
*Love is here, has always been here,*
*will be here forever.*
*The softest, quietest voice speaks inside,*
*'Love counts.*
*My love growing, regenerating*
*in you, in all things, could you but see it,*
***That's*** *what counts.'*

## 'At the end of the day'

### Creative

In 1 Corinthians 13, Paul concludes that whatever personal gifts he presents to Christ, he's nothing without love. Once ruled by the law, he's now ruled by love (Philippians 3:7–11). All is made possible once Paul recognises his chief desire: not to know about Christ, but to personally know Christ. By allowing the Holy Spirit to penetrate all his thoughts, experiences and actions, Paul can abandon himself to Love and then make love visible.

Spend some time now creatively pulling together what you've experienced in this section. Read 1 Corinthians 13 again, then return to the model or drawing you made earlier. Look at it lovingly, trying to see yourself again through God's eyes. Ask to claim a greater sense of God's eternal love in your thoughts,

...ree things remain: faith, hope and love

activities and relationships in ... when and where you're growing in ... ahead. Ask to recognise ... spite any challenges you face.

It may help to write down prayer requests ... aining to any issues you still have about faith, hope and love. To ... this, make three columns on a sheet of paper with the three headings: Faith, Hope, Love. Raise each prayer request to God. Write a reminder to yourself to check for answered prayer in the coming weeks.

Or you could write a love letter to God. This doesn't need to be expressed necessarily with overt emotions: just state simple intentions and desires to grow in the knowledge and love of God as feels right for you. End by thanking Jesus for speaking to you, in love. Take time to absorb the promise—that at the end of the day, however things look on earth right now, love will triumph over all.

# Emily Dickinson

*Andrea S[illegible]ington*

## Each life converges to some centre

### Introduction

Emily Dickinson (10 December 1830–15 May 1886)

*Each life converges to some centre*
*Expressed or still;*
*Exists in every human nature*
*A goal,*

*Admitted scarcely to itself, it may be,*
*Too fair*
*For credibility's temerity*
*To dare.*

*Adored with caution, as a brittle heaven,*
*To reach*
*Were hopeless as the rainbow's raiment*
*To touch,*

*Yet persevered toward, surer for the distance;*
*How high*
*Unto the saints' slow diligence*
*The sky!*

*Ungained, it may be, by a life's low venture,*
*But then,*
*Eternity enables the endeavouring*
*Again.*
608

We will be exploring some of the writing of this prolific and enigmatic Massachusetts poet, whose work was as fine and intricate as needlework, but whose subject matter was often unexpected. Her poems are rich in ambiguity, opening questions out to the reader; her words are coiled springs of meaning, with a life and energy of their own.

She was the daughter of a respected lawyer, from a comfortable home, and her early years appear quite conventional. She became increasingly uncomfortable with society, and with the emotional fervour of revivalism that swept through her community, and she became known in her later years as a recluse when she dressed in white, and stayed at home, usually seeing only a few close friends. However, she was a prolific correspondent, often sending poems to her friends. It was not until her death that the scale and breadth of her poetic output was discovered, and not until much more recently that her unconventional forms and subjects struck a deep chord in readers.

Emily Dickinson's work is best read with an open eye and mind, not rushing to understanding. Read it aloud if you can, listening as you would to music. Allow the images and words to rest in your imagination as you sit before God, developing the habit of pondering.

The poems are numbered following T.H. Johnson, *Emily Dickinson: The Complete Poems* (Faber, 1970).

# Listening for hope

## Reflective

*'Hope' is the thing with feathers—*
*That perches in the soul—*
*And sings the tune without the words—*
*And never stops—at all—*

*And sweetest—in the Gale—is heard—*
*And sore must be the storm—*
*That could abash the little Bird*
*That kept so many warm—*

*I've heard it in the chillest land—*
*And on the strangest Sea—*
*Yet, never, in Extremity,*
*It asked a crumb—of Me.*

254

This beautiful poem beguiles us with its simple hymn form, its interleaving rhymes and emphatic rhythm. We begin with 'the thing with feathers'—unnamed—mysterious, but the use of 'the' hints that it is something we already know. We listen to the bird of hope afresh, a voice beyond our everyday experience, reminding us of feathered angels. Emily Dickinson's distrust of conventional religious expression may be suggested by a 'tune without the words', as if she would listen to the bird's music without another's interpretation.

This poem reminds me of a time in the dead of winter, when, awake and troubled, I heard a robin sing outside my window in dazzling, frosty moonlight. It reminded me that night has light and beauty, and awakened hope.

So today, listen for unexpected sources of hope. It may be in the natural world, or in events, or people. Be especially careful to listen in your storms. Write them down, and they may become words to the song of hope God is singing to you daily.

## The little bird that kept so many warm

### Bible study/creative

Faith, hope and love (1 Corinthians 13:13) are key virtues in the Christian life. Of these, hope is the one we tend to neglect. It can seem too sweet, too prone to well-meaning platitudes, too unrealistic.

Looking at a concordance, or an online Bible search, we may be surprised to find how many references to hope there are in Job, and the darker psalms. Hope's place is in the storm. Fragile and feathered, it can withstand much that shakes us to the core. It is a way of being in the 'chillest' times. It seems to involve a confidence in the character of God—loving, patient and enduring—rather than in specific outcomes.

Read 'Hope' again, dwelling on the second two verses. Think of storms in your own life, and what has sustained you. Look for verses on hope in the Bible. You might like to try Job, Psalms (for example 42; 62), Romans (for example 5:4; 12:12), Ephesians (for example 1:18), or revisit significant passages from the previous section 'Three things remain: faith, hope and love'. Notice how tenacious hope is, and how it can grow in difficulties.

Draw or paint a response to the poem and your reading. You may want to include a bird and a storm, or you may not. As you draw freely, think of the things that sing hope in your life, that sustain you and help you hold on to God.

# Small acts of kindness and connection

## Creative

*They might not need me—yet they might—*
*I'll let my Heart be just in sight—*
*A smile so small as mine might be*
*Precisely their necessity.*

1391

Four lines, two rhyming couplets—short enough to remember. These words often return to me as I am about my daily business, gently opening my eyes to the people I overlook. It also reminds me of times I have received such a smile. It is deeply compassionate, and humble. It opens with a self-effacing 'They might not need me'—a hope that they will not, perhaps... but compassion corrects that, and shifts the focus to our necessity, our need, of another. In such a simple poem, the use of the word 'Heart' is striking: it is alarmingly vulnerable, a visible heart, softened by that 'just'. You can almost imagine the poet peeking out from behind a curtain, or a partially opened door. To let your heart be just in sight may be the balance we need between radical self-disclosure, which may be too much, and superficiality. It is a small honesty, like the small smile, which allows for the door of the heart to be opened wider in time.

Let this poem remind you to acknowledge those you meet today, recognising our common humanity. We never know how important a small connection, a gentle gesture, might be. Emily Dickinson used to leave gifts of flowers or home-baked bread for people in her community, accompanied by a poem. Perhaps you can give a small gift to someone. Seeking opportunities to connect and to bless, we find them. Practise the 'small smile'.

Try to pray a silent blessing over people as you walk past them, or remember them. Be open for a word to bless them with, like peace, or strength, or reconciliation, as the Spirit leads.

## The love a life can show below

### Going out

*The Love a Life can show below*
*Is but a filament, I know,*
*Of that diviner thing*
*That faints upon the face of Noon—*
*And smites the Tinder in the Sun—*
*And hinders Gabriel's Wing—*

*'Tis this—in Music—hints and sways—*
*And far abroad on Summer days—*
*Distils uncertain pain—*
*'Tis this enamours in the East—*
*And tints the Transit in the West*
*With harrowing Iodine—*

*'Tis this—invites—appals—endows—*
*Flits—glimmers—proves—dissolves—*
*Returns—suggests—convicts—enchants—*
*Then—flings in Paradise—*
673

This is a more mysterious, mystical poem, as suits its subject. Its beginning is simple—the 'I know' may suggest she is referring to a remark, or a conventional piety about how human love is a faint shadow of 'that diviner thing', but it soon moves on to word combinations and images that startle and dazzle.

The image of the love we can experience being a filament is striking enough, reminding us of the gauzy threads a spider spins seeking connection, the beginning of a web. These are faint hints of the greatness of God's love: 'For now we see in a mirror, dimly, but then we will see face to face. Now I know only in part; then I will know fully, even as I have been fully known' (1 Corinthians 13:12), Paul writes after his great paean to love. When we think the greatest love we have experienced on earth is but a filament of the love God has for us, we are awestruck.

Dickinson quickly moves on from Below, to this love that 'smites the Tinder in the Sun', the source and origin of all. Images of the sun burst through the rest of the poem, but they are not the 'diviner thing' itself, reminding us it is Christ in whom all things hold together (Colossians 1:15–17), and of the wonderful images of God in the Psalms.

Read Psalm 19:1–6, then spend some time considering the sky—particularly at sunrise and sunset. You may wish to go for a walk with a camera or some watercolours to focus your attention. I live in East Anglia, with its wide skies. Maybe you live far enough north to have witnessed the aurora borealis. Maybe you can study photographs of beautiful skies. Be open to what the heavens may be declaring. Think of the words in the first two stanzas—'Tinder', 'enamours', 'harrowing Iodine'—and find your own words to describe what you see and feel. Let your mind turn to God, behind all this, and express your response to God.

## 'In Music—hints and sways—'

### Creative

This small line breaks into the poem 'The Love a Life can show Below', introducing sound among the images of the sun. It is as if the line itself is hinting at something too—hinting at hinting. The association of ideas may suggest a heavenly music: the old idea of the music of the spheres, where the planets turn in a dance to music of their own making; or angelic music from beyond the stars, as we sway to the barely heard rhythms. It is certainly true that listening to music can help us to draw nearer to God; it can lift us, express things beyond words, move us to worship.

Give yourself time to listen to some music that moves and inspires you. It may be music you can sing to, or dance to, or play yourself. Allow the music to fill you and become praise, as you see God's beauty and majesty more clearly.

## Flings in paradise

### Creative

In the poem 'The Love a Life can show Below', after the extraordinary description of the evening sky as 'harrowing Iodine', a substance used to disinfect wounds, the poetic form breaks down in the final verse. The third ''Tis this' gives us a joyful and abundant list of verbs to describe God's revelation, the diviner love, that is hinted at in music, and enamours in sunrise. It demonstrates energy, and versatility: God is using any and every means to speak love into our lives, to bless and appal us into seeing God. I particularly love the juxtaposition of 'glimmers' and 'proves': one word so numinous, the other from the world of logic and science. All things are used by God to call us. As if all this is not enough, in the final line of the poem, 'Then—flings in Paradise—', there is something beyond what we see which is revealed: flung with abandon onto the top of the treasure pile. Paradise. Even this word is followed by a dash—as if there were more to come, or to give us a chance to catch our breath, and imagine what that might be.

Write out the verbs from the third ''Tis this' as a list in a column. Take each word in turn and, next to it, write things the word calls to mind. If one word speaks to you particularly, expand on that one theme. You may find your own poem emerging. Or think of ways of describing how God's love is revealed in your own life, and write your own list, repeating the process above. Offer what you write as a prayer, with thanks.

## It's all I have

### Reflective

*It's all I have to bring today—*
*This, and my heart beside—*
*This, and my heart, and all the fields—*
*And all the meadows wide—*
*Be sure you count—should I forget*
*Some one the sum could tell—*
*This, and my heart, and all the Bees*
*Which in the Clover dwell.*
26

This beautiful piece of modest generosity speaks of vulnerability. The one giving a gift is almost apologetic, but then, the gift giver reveals the abundance of what she is laying before the recipient. The poem follows a simple hymn structure and metre, interrupted by the insistent word 'this'—emphatically drawing attention to the gift. Most likely it is the poem itself, but we do not know. We do not know how the gift is received, but we know that it contains multitudes. It feels like an act of extravagant love, quietly spoken. There is a playful contrast, too, with the words borrowed from arithmetic—'count', 'one', 'sum' and 'tell'. She is expanding her 'all' to be truly all, and this causes us to think about the greatness of her 'this', and of the heart that comes with it, the wideness of the meadow, and the innumerable bees.

We have thought about giving small gifts—like a smile; now we think about receiving. The tiniest seeming gift from a person, or from God, can contain abundance. As I read this poem, I think of walking through the meadows near my home, astonished by the gift of light falling on the grasses, the splash of colour from the flowers. It can be hard to receive well, with delight, humility and gratitude. Today, notice good in what comes to you, and offer thanks to God.

## All things in their season

### Reflective/creative

*God made a little Gentian*
*It tried—to be a Rose—*
*And failed—and all the Summer laughed—*
*But just before the Snows*

*There rose a Purple Creature—*
*That ravished all the Hill—*
*And Summer hid her Forehead*
*And Mockery—was still—*

*The Frosts were her condition—*
*The Tyrian would not come*
*Until the North—invoke it—*
*Creator—Shall I—bloom?*

442

Emily Dickinson loved wild flowers, and had an extensive collection of botanically labelled pressed specimens (Susan VanZanten, *Mending a Tattered Faith,* Cascade Books, 2011, p. 30). We can imagine her seeing the elegant, cultivated women around her as roses, while she was a wild flower that did not bloom. As ever, it is not as simple as that. 'God made a little Gentian': she knows it has great worth. Maybe the frost that is necessary for the poet's flourishing is precisely the laughter of those around her, which must have made the solitude of her room and her table more appealing. The flower required the invocation—a deeply spiritual word—of the north wind to bloom.

Having told her parable, the poet applies it to herself. In the last line, is she seeking the Creator's invocation, permission even, to bloom? The line feels a little playful to me: yes, she is aware that her contemporaries do not know who she truly is, but the poem itself demonstrates that she knows herself. She knows that her work has the capacity to astonish and ravish, although not yet. It is not yet time for her.

So often we are impatient, and do not give ourselves the space and time and love to become who we truly are. We try to be roses, when gentians are even more astonishing. We rush too soon, and are discouraged too quickly.

Are there dreams you once had of blooming, that you have laid aside? Could the north wind be invoking you to flower when it seems too late? Could God be calling out your gifting now, with Moses, and Elizabeth, and Abraham?

Read Ecclesiastes 3:1–8 slowly, and lift your dreams and your days before God, asking for courage to bloom. You may wish to draw your image of some of the words, or pick a phrase and expand on it in your own writing. Look for good conditions to grow—what they are may surprise you.

# Possibility

## Creative/going out

*I dwell in Possibility—*
*A fairer House than Prose—*
*More numerous of Windows—*
*Superior—for Doors—*

*Of Chambers as the Cedars—*
*Impregnable of Eye—*
*And for an Everlasting Roof*
*The Gambrels of the Sky—*

*Of Visitors—the fairest*
*For Occupation—This—*
*The spreading wide my narrow Hands*
*To gather Paradise—*

657

Possibility seems a very fair house to be dwelling in—so different from the mundane and prosaic houses where windows and doors are few. For possibility to flourish in our lives, some things are needful. We need to be able to see out of our own constructed worlds into the light and wideness of the view beyond. We need doors through which we can easily walk, and which can be thrown open in fine weather to let in the sun and the breeze from beyond ourselves. This house of possibility is both self-contained and dependent on the outside.

Read Luke 11:34 about windows and doors.

Look out of the window—what do you see? Sit before your window and write or draw an impression of your view. Look carefully; what do you notice? Are there hints of possibility and adventure? Let your vision be sharpened; let your eye be full of light. Decide to take a different turn when you leave your house, so your own door is a gateway to a new possibility. Look for moments when the Spirit is leading and guiding you—wander, saunter, expect.

Pray that you will see possibilities God is bringing you.

# Everlasting roof

## Bible study/creative

The second verse of 'Possibility' begins with an ambiguous line: the plural 'Cedars' suggests the vast trees, which are strong and whose leaves provide 'impregnable' cover for hiding birds, but it is also a word rich in biblical resonance. Cedar was the wood used to both construct and line the temple, so it was a cedar chamber (1 Kings 6, especially v. 18). This house offers privacy, and deep sanctuary. The inner life can be a temple where the Spirit dwells (1 Corinthians 6:19), and this is something wonderful, something easily overlooked.

I love the description of the roof of the house of possibility—an 'Everlasting Roof'. Psalm 24 (King James Version) gives us 'everlasting doors', but here we have an infinite stretch of sky over the columns of cedars, so much more beautiful than a painted ceiling. 'Gambrels', a style of roof usually called mansard in the UK, allows height to rooms tucked away in the attic, with a wide, shallow slope at the highest point. It suggests capacity, possibly the Father's house with many rooms (John 14:2), or wide open blue.

Read Matthew 6:6 about prayer in the temple.

It is extraordinary to think that we are described as a temple—this is one of the great revelations of the Christian faith, that a human being can be the place where God dwells.

Read 1 Kings 6:14–38, taking in the richness of the description. Remember that you are such a temple, and the Spirit is within you. You might like to draw some of the things described. Remember how the cloud of God's presence filled the temple (1 Kings 8:10–11); ask that God's Spirit will fill you, and remain with you.

## Gathering paradise

### Meditative

The final verse of 'Possibility' shows that the house of possibility is, unsurprisingly, a place where things happen. The visitors are unnamed. We know that Emily Dickinson had few, but very close, friends. Her poems speak of birds and bees as if they were honoured guests, and some speak of angels, too. A fine collection of visitors! The last two lines are extraordinarily arresting. Her occupation: the gathering of paradise—what might that mean? Maybe paradise is spread around her, like manna, like daily life she turns to poems, like gifts of God's presence she apprehends. She is not limited by her narrow hands—they can spread wide for this.

Read Ephesians 3:17–20, and reflect on how this poem touches on many of these themes.

Consider your narrow hands gathering paradise. Study your hands. You might like to draw them, or draw round them. As you read verses 18–19 remember that your hands are able to span the immeasurable greatness of the love of Christ, and that this hand, and all of you, can be filled with that love. Allow this prayer to speak to you, to expand your awareness of the love and presence of Christ in your body, in your life.

# The presentation

*Janet Fletcher*

## Presentation

### Introduction

Read Luke 2:22–40.

In this section our thoughts and prayers will evolve from the passage found in Luke's Gospel recording the presentation of Jesus at the temple, which is celebrated on 2 February, or the nearest Sunday. Mary and Joseph followed the custom of their Jewish faith and so took Jesus, the firstborn, to be presented at the temple. No doubt they were surprised at all that happened next, and their meeting with Simeon and Anna.

Language and linguistics can be difficult. Some words have different meanings even though they have the same spelling! Some people can learn a new language easily while others find it difficult. I am in the latter group, as learning Welsh when coming to Wales, I discovered, is not as simple as I was led to believe!

Looking at the word 'presentation', or from that word, 'present', there are at least three different meanings and different ways of pronouncing it, each of which we shall encounter to bring into our prayer.

We 'present' ourselves before another person and reveal a part of the person we are, or not. A 'present' is a gift we give or receive. It can also mean, pronounced in the same way, being 'there', in the moment, at that time, and so being 'present' at some place.

The presentation of Jesus at the temple draws together each pronunciation and definition of the word 'present'.

What does the presentation of Christ at the temple say or mean to you—individually or as a church community? Is this feast day of the Church one that is celebrated in your church? It can be the day that turns us away from the birth of Jesus and towards the season of Lent and Christ's death on a cross.

# Come, Jesus, come

## Prayer

The following prayer can be prayed alone or within a group. Conclude your time of prayer with silence for reflection and further prayer, or silence or prayers could be offered after each bidding, to pray for personal requests, those of the local church, the wider community and the world.

*Come, Jesus, come, and illuminate our lives and this world with your Light,*
*In our cathedrals, churches, chapels and places of worship:*

**Come, Jesus, and illuminate them with your Light.**

*In our welcome of the stranger, the lonely, the elderly, and the young:*

**Come, Jesus, and illuminate them with your Light.**

*In prayer and worship offered, and the social gatherings of the community:*

**Come, Jesus, and illuminate them with your Light.**

*In times away, times alone, times with family, times with friends:*

**Come, Jesus, and illuminate them with your Light.**

*In the work we do or seek, and the leisure enjoyed:*
**Come, Jesus, and illuminate them with your Light.**

*In our striving to present you to the world around us, and the courage to stand firm in faith,*
*Come, Jesus, come, and illuminate our lives and this world with your Light:*
**Come, Jesus, and illuminate them with your Light.**

# Images and photographs

## Creative

Since having a digital camera I haven't had a single photograph printed. This may be because I don't know how to transfer them to the computer to print, and also because I take far fewer photographs! It all seemed a lot easier with a film that needed to be wound around within the camera and once finished was then taken to the appropriate place to be developed.

I do have many photographs of previous years. Some of these I don't mind looking at, while others make me cringe at the thought of having left the house wearing such clothes and hairstyles; they are, though, a statement of the time and year!

Do you have such photographs?

If the camera had been invented at the time of Jesus, what photographs would Mary and Joseph have taken? The presentation at the temple would no doubt be an occasion to record with a number of photographs. Or would it? For Mary it became an unexpected time of sorrow as well as of joy. Yet the photos we have embrace both: joyful and sorrowful memories. When you have time to pray, bring out your photograph albums and look through them.

What memories and feelings do they evoke?

Stay with the photos of loved ones who have died since that time; remember them and the times spent together.

Stay with the ones which remind you of times past, and perhaps forgotten.

If you can, make a collage of photographs taken from different years of your life.

Pray for those you encounter in your photograph albums.

Pray for the memories and photographs still to be taken.

## At the temple

### Imaginative

In a time and a space where you know you won't be disturbed, begin your prayer by slowly reading through Luke 2:22–40. This is a prayer where you can 'enter' into the story, in any way which feels comfortable to you. Once read, put aside your Bible and in your own way become still within, and then read through the meditation below a few times. It may be helpful to play quiet music in the background, or to light a small candle, as you seek to focus upon the presence of God with you and the movement of the Spirit.

Prayerfully imagine...

- the temple—what does it look like, its shape and size, its colours, shapes and sounds?
- the people—is it busy, noisy, quiet, who are the people, how are they dressed, what are they saying and doing?
- Simeon—where is he, what is he doing, what does he look like?
- Anna—where is she, what is she doing, what does she look like?

Then see Mary, Joseph and the baby Jesus as they enter the temple:

- What do they look like?
- Are they hesitant as they enter?
- What do they do?

Watch as Simeon and Anna move towards the Holy Family:

- What reaction, emotion, feelings are seen in their faces, the way they move?
- How do they approach the baby Jesus?

Is there anything you would like to say to Simeon, Anna, Joseph or Mary? Ask and allow the conversation to continue in your imagination.

As you end your prayer time, spend a few moments recalling...

- where you were in the temple
- how close to Simeon, Anna and the Holy Family you placed yourself
- what it felt like to be so close to the baby Jesus

When you are ready, draw this prayer to a close and give thanks to God. Then spend a little time reflecting upon how it felt, the story you were drawn into, the part you played, and make a note of everything you feel is important.

# 'Present'—our own self

## Reflective

The Christmas of my first year at theological college, my then young niece received a bead kit which meant she could make bracelets and necklaces. She made me a necklace which had in letter beads, 'My name is Aunty Janet'. This was then changed to 'My name is Janet'. I took this necklace back to college and hung it on the pinboard in my room as a reminder of who I am.

We present a different persona to different people. To my niece I was her aunty and so that needed to go on the necklace, but to others I am Janet, whether that was as 'daughter', or as 'sister', 'sister-in-law', 'friend', 'colleague' or 'vicar'. How I 'present' myself to each of them depends on which of those 'groups' they are a part of. I seek to be true to 'who I am', but reveal more to some than I do to others! Family know me well, but some friends know things family don't! This will be common to each of us.

Common to us all will be the way in which our personality, our characteristics, our likes and dislikes, our beliefs and faith, play a part in the way in which we present ourselves to others. Likewise the people we feel comfortable with, or uncomfortable with, and the friends and relationships we have. We can present a positive or a negative image of our self, which may or may not be true, or how others see us.

How would you describe yourself?

How true to your own self are you to the different groups of people you know?

Who knows you best?

Who can you be truly honest with, and so your true self?

This leads us to the question of which part of ourselves we present to God: all or some? How open and honest are we when we come to God in prayer? How we present ourselves to God often relates to the image of God we have: a God who is approachable or distant, who loves unconditionally or only if we 'do well and achieve'.

What is your image of God?

How may prayer help you to present yourself more openly and honestly to God, and to friends, family and colleagues?

## The 'after-effect'

### Imaginative

*Simeon and Anna looked at each other. They stood alone, together, within the crowd, alone with their thoughts that could not be put into speech. The hustle and bustle of people passing by did not disturb them.*

*The seeming eternity of their silence was only broken when hesitantly they both murmured as one, 'It has all come to pass.' Only then could their voices begin to proclaim their deepening understanding and joy, and the reality of all that had taken place before their eyes.*

*As they stood looking at each other, they remembered how separately they had watched and waited, each in their own part of the temple. They had seen each other in the distance, unaware of how their paths would cross. Separately they had each been drawn to the baby held with love in his mother's arms. Separately they had reached the One they had long waited for.*

*Now as they stood together, they knew they had shared something very special. Together they had shared in the wonder of meeting with the Holy Family. Together they had shared in the prophecy spoken out loud as Jesus was presented at the temple, a prophecy which would bring both joy and sorrow. Together they had witnessed the emotions which had passed through the eyes of Mary as she heard the prophecy spoken, the sword of pain drawn close.*

*Together they shared in this long-awaited experience of divine love, presented to them by God. Together they could rejoice and reveal the mystery of the incarnation to the world, and to all who had ears to hear. This day, long watched for, hoped for and anticipated, had entered into their lives. This day would change each of their lives, separately and together.*

*Now, as they looked at each other, they each knew that they could go and proclaim the wonder of God to all who would listen. They also knew that they could both now go in peace.*

What experiences of life and faith have changed your life?

Which of these experiences have been shared with others?

How have times of joy and of sorrow shaped your life?

Who do you share these times and experiences with, if you do share them?

## Nunc dimittis

### Prayer

In the Gospel of Luke we read the words of Simeon:

> *'Master, now you are dismissing your servant in peace,*
> *according to your word; for my eyes have seen your salvation,*
> *which you have prepared in the presence of all peoples,*
> *a light for revelation to the Gentiles and for glory to your people Israel.'*
>
> LUKE 2:29–32, NRSV

These words are a part of the conversation and prophecy Simeon spoke to Mary. Within the Anglican Church, these words of Simeon, albeit slightly altered, are to be found in the liturgy for evensong; in Cranmer's evening prayer as well as in more modern translations. These are words which have travelled through the ages.

Ignatian spirituality calls us to look back and review all that has been. Ignatius named it the 'Examination of Consciousness', which may seem both difficult and complicated, but is the honest review of the day or week or month or year. Very simply, it is to reflect upon where God has, or hasn't, been present in our time and life.

In the evening and night we are 'dismissed' in peace. We are called to look back on our day for moments of God's salvation, and the light of Christ in the day we have journeyed through.

A prayer for the night-time and before we sleep:

*O God, as I come to sleep this night,*
*watch over me, and those who I love and know.*
*Open my heart and eyes to all that has taken place this day,*
*in my own life and across this world;*
*which I remember before you now…*

Quietly review the day, and give particular thanks for one special moment of the day.

*O God, for times and memories of joy, thank you.*
*For times of sorrow and despair, be with me.*
*Be my salvation as you are the salvation of the world.*
*Prepare within me the possibilities of the coming day,*
*that I may be open to and embrace all*
*you may ask of me, and call me towards,*
*in the new day to come. Amen*

# 'Present'—a gift

## Reflective

At this time of the year the gift giving of Christmas is behind us, and unless we are well prepared in the January sales, the gift buying is far enough away for us not to think about it too much! Through the year there will be gifts to give on birthdays and for an anniversary. These may not be the only occasions when we present a gift to someone.

Right now, it may be we are still counting the cost of Christmas, or it may be that a manageable budget was set and kept to. The shops, all year round, entice us to spend and spend even more. If we give a present, a gift, to another person, we do not need to spend a small fortune. Often, it is the 'cheapest' of gifts, and especially ones that are home-made, home-crafted, which are the most loved and cherished.

What are the most cherished gifts you have received? And why?

The presentation of Jesus at the temple draws to a close the Christmas and Epiphany season, and we are called to turn around and look towards Lent. From the gift of a newborn child, fulfilling the prophecy from centuries before, we move to the coming gift of Jesus, giving himself upon a cross for each and every one of us.

We have received the gift of God revealed to us and taking on human form and flesh. In the year of the Church, we soon begin to look ahead to the gift of the Holy Spirit and eternal life. From God we have received the present of faith, and are blessed with many and varied gifts. Yet, for a present to reveal what lies inside, it needs to be opened, its wrappings ripped off.

What are the gifts God has given you as a present, a present to be shared?

What can you offer as a present to the church community and to the wider community?

# Presence

## Going out

Our times of prayer do not need to be confined to sitting in church, or at home, alone or with others. Prayer can be offered in many different ways. One way is to go out for a walk—around where you live, or further afield. You can pray during a ramble, a short or long walk, or while out jogging or running. A prayer of awareness to all that is around you, and a seeking and praying for God's presence within and with the places you pass.

Decide where your prayer walk will be. Can you simply step out from your front door, or is further preparation required as travel to that place is included?

Begin by offering the time to God.

Ask for awareness of the surroundings so that you can be present to the various sights, sounds and scents.

As you walk, jog or run, hold in prayer the houses, the places of work, the open spaces of creation, and the people you pass. Ask God to be present in love and peace.

At the end of your time on this prayer walk, perhaps when you have returned home, spend some time reflecting upon all you have seen. Give thanks to God for all you have been aware of and prayed for during that time.

# 'Present'—to be there

## Reflective

How quickly do you become bored? How soon do you become frustrated at the 'slowness' of a meeting? At which point do you let your mind wander? Our body is physically present but our attention has drifted to another place.

I am probably now known for doodling on agendas and notes of meetings, filling in the circles and then making shapes around the words. But that doesn't mean I'm not listening!

To be present, to be there and remain attentive to all that is taking place, can at times be extremely easy or extremely difficult. To be present in this way will be a part of our working life, our hobby and leisure time, and the time we spend in prayer with God.

When we seek to be present with God in quiet prayer, this is usually the time our minds are filled with numerous distractions. It can take time and practice to put aside incoming thoughts so we can simply be there with God.

Attentiveness to the surroundings in which we are at that moment present can either be conducive to quiet prayer or the very opposite.

To be present with God, or another person, requires attentiveness, listening deeply. In prayer, or in gathered worship, what helps you to be present in that moment and attentive?

In prayer, or in gathered worship, what distracts or frustrates you, or makes you feel bored and so inattentive and not present?

Where is the place where you can find the quietness to be present with God?

Go to that place and spend some time being present with God. Practise putting aside the distractions and returning to focus on God.

# Mary

## Meditative

In a place where you can be quiet and undisturbed, a place to be present with God, become comfortable and still within, in your own way.

Mary goes to the temple to be purified after childbirth, as well as to present her firstborn son. Women after childbirth were declared as being unclean and so needed the temple priest to offer the rite of purification. Up until the last half of the 20th century it was common for women to go to their church for 'churching', to be declared 'clean' and so able to go out with their baby and visit family and friends.

How did it feel to Mary, and other women, to be considered unclean because of childbirth?

Mary followed the Jewish traditions. As a woman she was limited in where she could go or what she could do within the temple. As she looked at the baby she held, what thoughts ran through her mind? How did the meeting with Simeon and Anna really affect her? Maybe this was the moment when she realised what her 'Yes' to the angel Gabriel was truly to mean.

How may Mary have felt, knowing she had been called to bring to birth God's Son, but could not fully partake in the life and worship of the temple?

Whatever thoughts she pondered over and kept in her heart, she never gave up. Mary must have been far more than the 'mother mild' image given to her from the Christmas carol. She must have been a woman of strength and courage, of love and compassion. Mary had to let her son go, to follow his very particular call as the Son of God, and then follow him to the foot of the cross.

Spend some time reflecting on your own call from God. Does that call need you to be strong and courageous, loving and compassionate? Re-offer that call to God, or ask for clarity in how he is calling you.

## Drawing all together

### Creative

Over the past days we have drawn into our thoughts and prayers the word 'present'. It is a word which embraces different meanings and different ways of being pronounced.

Recall the different ways the word 'present' has been used, and how it touches upon, maybe challenges, our relationship with God and our journey of faith.

It may be helpful to write down on a large piece of paper, or in a journal, the word 'present' and then to add around it, for example, the different interpretations, the different challenges you have faced, a call from God to use your gifts and giftedness, words or phrases from times of prayer, or from the Bible passage in Luke. Include, also, any particular ways of prayer you might like to look at further, and the commitment to seek a deeper attentiveness in prayer, worship and your surroundings.

For Mary and Joseph, the journey continued season by season. Together they watched over Jesus as he grew and became strong, filled with wisdom and the favour of God which rested upon him.

*God of love,*
*when I feel weak, help me grow strong,*
*in times of decision making, fill me with wisdom,*
*when I feel distracted, guide my attentiveness,*
*in times of doubt and struggle, deepen my faith,*

*and in all things may I offer my gifts in your name,*
*for you are present with me always,*
*in Jesus Christ and the Holy Spirit. Amen*

# The practice of the presence of God

*Sally Smith*

## Who was Brother Lawrence?

### Introduction

Nicholas Herman was born in Hériménil in Lorraine in France in the 17th century. He was a man of lowly birth who became a soldier, probably in his teens. He was injured near the small town of Rambervillers and it is thought that he then left the army with a permanent disability. He became a footman, and not a particularly successful one by his own account.

At some point later in his life he was accepted as a lay brother into the order of Discalced Carmelites. It was there that he began developing his 'practice of the presence of God', which forms the title of the only record of his life. The book was written and put together by M. Beaufort, grand vicar to M. de Chalons, formerly Cardinal de Noailles. It is available free online, though there are different translations and you may find more modern language used in print versions. The book consists of a series of conversations held over a period of 15 months and letters sent over a period of ten years, giving spiritual advice. Some versions also include the principles and ways that Brother Lawrence held and advocated. The book is short and clear in the simple message that is repeated throughout in both the letters and the conversations. I therefore make no apologies if we seem to cover the same material in different ways. Brother Lawrence maintains his one message; in one of his letters he says, 'You will tell me that I am always saying the same thing to you. It is true, and I do not know a better and easier means than that. And since I practise no other, I urge it upon everybody. We must know before we love, and to know God we must often think of him' (p. 52).

He took the name of Brother Lawrence and spent most of his time in the monastery in the kitchen—not ideal for someone described as 'a big heavy-handed man who broke everything'. But in the kitchen he learned to practise being in God's presence and worshipping him in the everyday jobs.

It was his way to use 'visible things to reach the invisible'. Throughout the book are various images and we shall look at these as we learn from his teaching and follow in his way.

To begin with, here are a few quotes from Brother Lawrence:

> ... our sole business in this life is to please God...
>
> p. 51

> What can God have that gives him greater satisfaction than that a thousand times a day all his creatures should pause to withdraw and worship him in the heart.
>
> p. 69

> We must not grow weary in doing little things for the love of God, who looks not to the greatness of the deed, but to the love.
>
> p. 30

> It is only necessary to realise that God is intimately present within us, to turn at every moment to him and ask for his help, recognise his will in all things doubtful, and to do well all that which we clearly see he requires of us, offering

> what we do to him before we do it, and giving thanks for having done it afterwards.
>
> p. 29

# Arising from faith

## Creative

Brother Lawrence advocates moments of worship of God throughout the day. This is not because he believes we ought to do this, or because God requests it. It arises from who Brother Lawrence believes God to be, and for him it happens as a natural response to God.

> All these acts of worship must arise from faith, and the belief that in truth God is in our hearts; that we must worship him, love him and serve him in spirit and in truth; that he sees all that which comes to pass, and that will come to pass, in us and in all his creatures; that he exists apart from everything, and is the one on whom all other creatures depend, that he is infinite in all perfection and merits by his boundless excellence and sovereign power all that which we are, and that which is in heaven and on earth, all of which he can dispose at his good pleasure in time and eternity.
>
> p. 70

Brother Lawrence tells us what he believes about God that makes him want to worship him and be in his presence continually. This will be different for each of us, as we each know (and are known) in our own unique way.

Try writing a passage that explains what you believe about who God is. What is it about God that underlies all that you are and do? How does this make you want to be in his presence continually and to worship him throughout the day? It is likely it will be completely different from what Brother Lawrence wrote, and you may well find you keep adding to it and altering it.

When you are ready, stop and slowly read what you have written. As you read, notice the response that occurs within you. What do you find yourself wanting to do as you read it? Give yourself the time to respond as appropriate.

## Treasure

### Imaginative

Brother Lawrence uses treasure to describe how precious God's love and presence within a person is:

> ... what contentment and satisfaction he enjoys, conscious, as he is, of so great a treasure within him. He is no longer anxious about finding it; he has not the trouble of seeking it; he is free to take what he pleases of it.
>
> p. 36

> How happy we should be if we could find the treasure of which the Gospel speaks. The rest would seem nothing to us. Since it is boundless, the more we dig, the more wealth we find there. Let us ceaselessly search for it. Let us not grow weary until we have found it...
>
> p. 47

Brother Lawrence is saying that what we value most is closest to our hearts and it is that which we turn to and notice regularly. What we love, we think of often. The more we love, the more we think and remember. Also, God's love for us is boundless, and so the more we seek and search for it, the more of it we find.

Imagine holding a beautiful chest; see how well it is decorated, feel the quality of the workmanship. Turn it and look at it from different sides.

This is a valuable chest and deserves to hold only the most valuable of items. As you hold it, what do you want to keep in here? What is valuable enough to be worthy of being held in such a beautiful casket? Notice your first thought in answer to that question, and see if it changes as you think about it further.

Imagine opening your treasure chest and putting in your greatest treasures. Cherish each as you carefully place it inside.

Then invite God to add another treasure. Ask what he wants to put in. This may be something you already have but haven't included, or it may be a gift he wishes to give to you. Do you allow him to add his treasure?

Throughout the rest of the day, remember that chest and the treasure it contains, particularly God's contribution. Allow the treasure to draw you closer to him.

## Picking up straws

### Creative

In his third conversation, and again in the fifth letter, Brother Lawrence refers to picking up straws for the love of God. He would gladly pick up a straw if that were what God had asked him to do. He would do it because of his love for God. In 17th-century France there would have been plenty of straws to pick up, and it would not necessarily have been Brother Lawrence's job to pick them all up, but the end of each action was the love of God; that was his motive for all he did.

Walk around your house and look for bits on the floor—it's not likely to be straw, but look for the bits of fluff and leaves and other rubbish that end up in our homes. Each one you see, bend over and pick it up—not through a sense of duty, but because God will be delighted with each one. As you pick a piece up, acknowledge it to God—notice his thanks and appreciation of what you are doing. See his value placed on your action with the tiny pieces we usually ignore, or leave to the vacuum cleaner to remove.

Throughout the day keep your eyes on the floor and begin to notice other bits that need to be picked up. Bend down and please God with your action. You might want to tell him about each one you notice. Listen to what he says to you. Notice if there is any shifting in the relationship between you and God.

## Savour small moments

### Reflective

> ... pause for some short moment, as often indeed as we can, to worship God in the depth of our heart, to savour him, though it be in passing, as it were by stealth. Since you are not unaware that God is present before you whatever you are doing, that he is at the depth and centre of your soul, why not then pause from time to time at least from that which occupies you outwardly, even from your spoken prayers, to worship him inwardly, to praise him, petition him, to offer him your heart and thank him?
>
> p. 69

God delights in our attention. He loves it when we notice him. Is there someone you love so much that you can just enjoy being with them? You don't need to do anything, just be together in the ordinary everyday. Or is there someone to whom you mean so much that they enjoy having you around, doing day-to-day tasks and pastimes? Think about those relationships and how much just being together and being acknowledged means. Stay with the importance of those moments together and how they impact on the one who loves.

God loves us infinitely more than anyone humanly can. He delights in our presence. He longs for those moments when we acknowledge he is with us. He doesn't berate us for our failure to notice him, but cherishes the moments when we do. He doesn't expect us to be ceaselessly focused on him—he knows we can't live in this world and be constantly turned to him—but he loves it when we do focus. As young lovers are excited by a text message in the middle of the day, so God is excited by our turning to glance at him, to recognise that he is still there, with us and waiting for that stolen glance, that secret moment with him.

> He does not ask much of us—an occasional remembrance, a small act of worship, now to beg his grace, at times to offer him our distresses, at another time to render thanks for the favours he has given, and which he gives in the midst of your labours, to find consolation with him as often as you can... The smallest remembrance will always please him. It is not needful at such times to cry aloud. He is nearer to us than we think.
>
> p. 41

So, as you go about your activity today, pause for a second to look at God. Don't talk; just offer him a loving glance. You may be aware of him looking back at you, or his love and watchfulness of you. Or you may just acknowledge him and continue with what you are doing. Remember the pleasure each glance will give him.

Brother Lawrence later suggests that if we practise this acknowledging of God's presence during the day, it will be easier to 'remain quiet during your prayers, or at least recall the mind from its straying' (p. 50). Our mind becomes used to looking for God and to returning to him after distraction.

## Paralytic

### Imaginative

> I do not advise you do much talking at prayer, for much talking is often an occasion for wandering. Hold yourself before God as a dumb person, or a paralytic at a rich man's gate. Give your attention to keeping your mind in the presence of the Lord.
>
> p. 50

Next time you are praying using words, notice how much your mind wanders. Some people find words useful to focus their mind and help them to pray. Others find words are a distraction that draw them away from God. Neither is right or wrong, but notice how you are made. Whether words help or hinder, it can be good to pray both with and without words.

Brother Lawrence gives us the image of a poor person, unable to speak, or someone unable to move, sitting or lying by a rich man's gate. Presumably they are waiting for the rich person to pass by and offer them money or food. They will need to communicate with the rich benefactor without words or actions. How would you do this? As you sit, imagine you can neither move nor talk. How will you express to God your love for him? How will you acknowledge his presence with you? Allow him to gaze at you, as you gaze at him. Relax and receive his peace, for he doesn't want you to be distressed. Nothing matters in this moment but being in the presence of God. Enter into a 'wordless and secret conversation between soul and God' (p. 44). Stay there as long as you can.

When you return, notice how you feel and what thoughts begin to enter your head. Thank God that he is always willing to spend time with you.

## Fire of sacred love

### Going out/creative

> ... this gentle loving gaze of God insensibly lights a fire divine in the soul, which so warmly kindles it with the love of God that one is constrained to temper it with so many outward acts.
>
> p. 74

> Hope imbues the will with a scorn for earthly things and kindles it with the fire of sacred love, because, being always with God who is consuming fire, it burns to ashes whatever stands against it. This soul, thus kindled, can only go on living in the presence of its God, a presence which engenders in its heart a holy ardour, a sacred eagerness and longing to see this God loved, known, served and worshipped by all creatures.
>
> p. 77

The divine fire can be a gentle flame that burns within, giving light and warmth and the comfort those who have a fire at home will recognise. But God is also a consuming fire, destroying and burning to ashes.

Light a fire out of doors. If you are not used to doing this, you could use an old baking tray, or the base of the barbecue. You could use a tea light and add some small twigs as it burns. But remember, fire is not always gentle; you may want to have water nearby just in case.

As the fire begins to burn, watch it consume the twigs and sticks you feed it with. Watch the flames dance and see how they are moved and fanned by the wind. Feel the heat.

Notice the different phases of your fire, from the first vulnerable delicate flames to the roaring, consuming fire. See it die down and lose its strength. See how you interact with it in the different stages, nurturing, coaxing, feeding, fearing, watching, giving and receiving.

Allow God's 'fire of sacred love' to be kindled in you. Use what you have learnt about fire to kindle and enable this love to grow.

After the fire has died down, you may want to spend some time with the ashes. How do you feel as you clear up? What do you want for the ashes?

## The winter tree

### Going out

Brother Lawrence describes his conversion at the age of 18. He was looking at a bare winter tree and began thinking about the time when it would be covered with leaves and flowers and fruits, and then about the provider God who would do this work. This drew him into such great love for God that he was not sure if this increased at all in the rest of his life.

Go outside and find somewhere to sit where you can look at a bare tree. Notice the branches, hidden for so much of the year by leaves. Look at the shapes and colours.

Then begin to accept that soon these branches will begin to grow leaves, and then flowers and fruit.

Recognise the power of the provider who creates these good gifts.

Allow this vision of providence to draw you away from the world and towards God.

Let bare branches you see over the coming days turn you back to God.

## Breaking down dams

### Imaginative/reflective

> We are blind who so bind the hands of God, and we stem the abundance of his grace.
>
> p. 36

Brother Lawrence recognises that we are often satisfied with the crumbs from God when he has so much more to offer to us. We settle for a bit when we could have loads. He suggests we dam the torrential stream of God's flowing grace, and he asks Reverend Mother N. (to whom this letter is written) to break down the dam and to open the way for God's grace. He says we are to be pitied for being satisfied with so little when God has such treasures to give us.

Visit a reservoir with a dam, or find some images of dams online. Sense the power of the water and the strength of the dam in keeping that water back.

How much strength do you put into holding back the power of God? Recognise the ways in which you block God.

Imagine what would happen if a dam broke, or look for images online. See the power of the water set free. If that power could be used for good, what could it do? The dam doesn't have to be removed all in one go. To keep the water from causing damage it can be reduced slowly and the water allowed to flow gently away; you may find images of this happening.

As you watch, notice what dams you have inside and ask God for help in gently removing those dams and allowing him to work.

> When he finds a soul imbued with living faith, into it he pours grace on grace, a flowing stream, as it were, which, checked in its proper course, and finding a new outlet, spreads wide with force, abundantly.
>
> p. 36

## Sail on

### Reflective

> Those who have the mind of the Holy Spirit sail on, even when they are asleep. If the small ship of our soul is still beaten by the winds and the storm, let us awaken the Lord who sleeps in it, and he will soon calm the sea.
>
> p. 37

The Celtic form of Compline from the Northumbria Community uses the imagery of lying down with God, sleeping with God and awaking with God, inviting God as Father, Son and Spirit to be with the pray-er as they sleep and as they wake.

Saying a brief form of Compline before going to bed is one way of committing your sleep to God and inviting him to be present with you during the night.

Another is to take a 'holding cross' to bed with you. It's surprising how it can remain in your hand throughout the night as you hold on to God (or he holds on to you).

Consider how you can continue to sail with God as you sleep.

# Making a sculpture

## Creative

> Sometimes I think of myself as a piece of stone before its sculptor, from which he intends to make a statue. Setting myself thus before God, I beg him to shape his perfect image in my soul, and to make me exactly like him.
>
> p. 46

Take a bar of soap and a small knife and begin to sculpt. You may have an image in mind you want to create, or you may just experience carving and creating.

As you work, notice how easily the soap cuts and forms into new shapes. Watch the shavings fall. Smell the scent released as you cut.

Allow yourself to feel how God shapes you as you shape the soap. As you delight in your creation, sense God's delight in his creation. As the soap yields and takes on new shapes, let God mould and shape you.

We are not perfect sculptors. Whatever your skill, delight in your creation. How much greater is God's delight in his creation as he shapes us into his perfect image!

You could use your soap, and watch as the hands and water it encounters continue to shape it. Or you might like to keep it in your prayer space and let the scent fill you afresh.

# Practising

## Creative

The version of *The Practice of the Presence of God* that I have been using finishes with some principles and ways which sum up the recommendations Brother Lawrence has made in his letters and conversations.

He wants his readers to find joy in God, to recognise they are in his company and that he delights in their company.

Brother Lawrence asks them to do everything for God with thoughtfulness and consideration.

He tells them to pause for short moments.

God loves us and loves to spend time with us. He loves it when we stop and notice him; when we say we love him. Loving God liberates us from self-love and all the things that destroy us.

Brother Lawrence is realistic and recognises his readers' need to get on with everyday life, as he did in the kitchen of the monastery, so his suggestions are possible in everyday life.

What has been the main message you have received from Brother Lawrence?

Brother Lawrence's letters were letters of advice to other Christians. If you were to write a letter of advice to another Christian now, what would you say? Try writing it.

When you have finished, sit down and read your letter as if it were written to you. Receive the advice contained in the letter.

You might return regularly to the letter to receive your advice again.

Our sole business in this life is to please God.

p. 51

We cannot avoid the dangers and the reefs of which this life is full, without the real and constant help of God. Let us ask him for it without ceasing. But how can we ask him without being with him? And how can we be with him without often thinking of him? And how can we often think of him without forming a holy habit of doing so?

p. 51

All quotations are from the book *The Practice of the Presence of God: Brother Lawrence*, translated by E.M. Blaiklock (Hodder & Stoughton, 1981).

# Shaping Lent: Matthew 1—7

*Helen Julian CSF*

## According to Matthew

### Introduction

Matthew is going to be our companion throughout Lent, so a good start would be to see what we can learn about him, and the Gospel which bears his name. Begin by reading something you may always have skipped—the genealogy in Matthew 1:1–17.

What is immediately obvious is that this is a very Jewish Gospel; the whole genealogy is designed to link Jesus into the people of the covenant, to show how he fulfils God's promises to his people. Matthew often quotes the Old Testament to show how Jesus fulfils its prophecies, for example 1:22–23; 2:5–6, 15, 17–18, 23; 3:3 and 4:14–16. As you'd expect, most of the genealogy runs from father to son—but there are five breaks in this, one in verse 11 where Josiah was 'the father of Jeconiah and his brothers'; and the others where women appear in the story—Tamar, Rahab, Ruth, and the wife of Uriah. Even God's plans don't always work out quite as anticipated.

But the Gospel doesn't stand on its own; 55 per cent of it also appears in Mark, which the writer of Matthew probably had to hand as he wrote. There are also overlaps with Luke. It's likely it was written towards the end of the first century, at a time, after the destruction of the temple in Jerusalem, when Judaism was in flux, and Matthew's community of Jewish Christians was also seeking to find its place, deciding if they were one group within Judaism, or if they needed to break away. So the Gospel focuses on questions especially relevant to Jewish Christians, hence the stress on how Jesus fulfils the Old Testament promises.

If he is the fulfilment of promise, then he is to be believed and above all obeyed. It's a very Jewish emphasis on action—on doing the right thing over getting the doctrine right.

Most of us probably have a favourite Gospel—which is yours? And if it's not Matthew, how do you feel about spending Lent with this Gospel?

## Strive for the kingdom

### Reflective

How are your New Year's resolutions doing? Two months into the new year, if you're anything like me, many of them have moved gently into the background of life, with just the odd twinge of guilt to remind me of my good intentions. The beginning of Lent is a time when many Christians make new resolutions for the season—and often with the same disappointing results. Perhaps Matthew can offer us some help.

Read Matthew 6:19–21 and 25–33 slowly. As you read, notice what words or phrases especially attract you. These verses are not so much about doing particular things, but about an entire attitude to life, and maybe that's the key to real change.

Lent, the period between Ash Wednesday and Easter Sunday, began as a period of intensified effort for new Christians as they reached the end of their preparation for baptism at Easter. It echoed Jesus' 40 days in the wilderness immediately after his own baptism, where he wrestled with his calling. Soon this holy time was taken up by existing Christians too in solidarity with their soon-to-be brothers and sisters in faith. Baptism then was a life-changing decision, affecting every aspect of life, and often causing real dilemmas in family and work life.

These verses challenge us to consider our priorities, assuring us that if we put God and God's work first, our other needs will also be met. Sit quietly with the words which struck you. Repeat them slowly, allowing them to become part of you, to settle somewhere deep inside you. Allow them to change you. Notice how you feel as you hear them. Spend time with the words. You may want to write them down and keep them where you'll notice them as a reminder of their power.

What would it look like to 'strive first for the kingdom of God' (v. 33, NRSV)? It may be something quite small—for me, making sure that I have prayer time before starting work, and making time for serious reading even when other work seems pressing. It's all part of making 'treasures in heaven' my priority, and aligning my heart and my choices with that. Can you find the one choice you can make this Lent which would express that desire for you?

## Whenever you pray

### Bible reading

Read Matthew 6:5–15; if you have time, extend this to 6:2–18.

Prayer, fasting and almsgiving, the three topics from this passage, were taken for granted as religious practices, both for Jews and the early Christians. We can see this simply from Jesus' words 'whenever you pray', 'whenever you give alms', 'whenever you fast'. He doesn't need to convince his disciples to take up something new. For the early Church these were the three best ways to obtain forgiveness of sins, and we can see this spelt out in this passage in relation to prayer.

The section about prayer is far longer than the other two. The sections on almsgiving and fasting simply instruct, whereas here Matthew includes the example of a prayer which Jesus gives his disciples—the Lord's Prayer. It was common for rabbis to compose prayers for their disciples to use; the simplicity and brevity of this prayer reinforces Jesus' injunction not to 'heap up empty phrases' (v. 7, NRSV).

Such a famous passage has of course been much commented on, and commentators differ on how to interpret it. Is it a prayer for the age to come, or for now? Is it given as an example of how to pray, or as an exact formula to be repeated word for word? Perhaps one of the best places to start is with the verse immediately before the prayer, 'for your Father knows what you need before you ask him'. Here is a clear statement that the purpose of words in prayer is to help us to articulate our desires and concerns, and not to inform God.

It's possible to see the prayer as including both of the dimensions above—the now and the coming kingdom; and to be both an example of prayer and a gift of words when our own fail. The first three petitions are focused on the kingdom of God, a central concern of Matthew; then the focus shifts to human needs—the basic need of nourishment; for reconciliation with one another, which enables reconciliation with God; and for salvation at the time of judgement, and protection from all that is evil.

Use the prayer daily over the next week. Allow the words to nourish and inform the rest of your prayer.

## Whenever you give alms

### Reflective

Read Matthew 6:2–4.

We may see prayer and fasting as specifically religious acts, with almsgiving a less religious virtue. Many would be more likely to call it charitable giving, everything from a few coins in the collecting tin to the charitable foundations set up by Bill Gates and Mark Zuckerberg. But for early Christians almsgiving had a very high status—a mid-second-century sermon placed the three practices of prayer, fasting and almsgiving in that order, with almsgiving as the most valuable.

Early Christian writers had genuine doubts as to whether it was possible to be rich and a Christian, and although they generally concluded that it was, this was only acceptable if the rich used their wealth to aid the poor. In return the poor prayed for those who helped them—and hence in an interesting reversal it was the rich who benefited the most from the almsgiving.

Augustine wrote that 'whatever you have in excess is not your own property'—a thought-provoking idea for most of us. In comparison to those in need in our own country, let alone in other parts of the world, how much of what you own is essential, and what is 'in excess'?

As you look around your home, and at your diary and yourself, identify some excesses—this could be money, time, talents, possessions. How might you pass this on to someone to whom it would be essential? In the early Church, almsgiving was compared to baptism itself and seen as a means of cleansing sin committed after baptism. Baptism could not be repeated, but almsgiving could. So as you give away your excess, allow God to cleanse and renew you. Remember, Paul wrote, 'God loves a cheerful giver' (2 Corinthians 9:7). How might you give more joyfully, of whatever you have in excess—money, time, talents—this Lent?

# Whenever you fast

## Reflective

Read Matthew 6:16–18.

The pattern is familiar—the assumption that Jesus' hearers *will* give alms, pray and fast; instructions about what not to do, and what to do; and an assurance that what is done in the right way will be rewarded by God.

This instruction is probably aimed at fasting over and above that which was undertaken communally in the Jewish world: simply joining in, which would have attracted no particular kudos. But additional fasting, perhaps undertaken as an accompaniment to prayer, could be an opportunity to draw attention to oneself, to be seen as especially holy, in the same way as flamboyant almsgiving, or ostentatiously public prayer.

Fasting today can be undertaken for entirely unreligious reasons, as part of a diet or health regime. It's interesting to speculate whether that makes fasting for religious reasons easier or more difficult. Is it being hypocritical to allow others to assume that you are fasting for health reasons if your motivation is actually religious? Or is it a way of fasting in secret? There's no obvious answer—what do you think?

Of course it's possible to fast from things other than food—perhaps a reflection of our world of plenty is the number of choices we have as to how to exercise this discipline. Some people choose to 'fast' from social media for Lent, from specific kinds of food or drink, or from particular entertainment. Some will link their fasting (especially if it saves money) with generosity, giving the money saved to projects helping those in need. Again there may be a conflict between the desire to publicise the fasting to encourage others to participate, and the desire to gain the secret reward that comes from fasting only in the eyes of God.

How might fasting be a part of your Lent, and how can it be done in the spirit of today's reading? Remember, it doesn't have to be for the whole of Lent. You could begin with one day, or maybe try one day a week.

# Repent...

## Creative

Read Matthew 3:1–6.

Here John the Baptist makes his first appearance in this Gospel. He is a striking figure, dressed in camel's hair and with an unusual diet. He is very clear about his message—'repent'. This can sound a harsh injunction with overtones of severe judgement and disapproval. But the heart of repentance is turning—turning away from the wrong path and turning back to the right one. It ought to be a life-giving part of the Christian life, as we follow the satnav of our conscience and 'turn around as soon as possible'.

Find a creative way of expressing your desire to 'turn', to repent. You may use words, writing your own liturgy, with a regular refrain, such as 'I turn back to you, O God'. You may choose to use colour, shape and images, in paint or collage. Your image doesn't need to represent what you are repenting of (though it may); it could speak of your sense of being separated from God, and the joy of return. Or you might use your body in dance or sacred movement.

If you choose to be creative in a way which leaves you with something on paper, give some thought to what you will do with it. Will you destroy it, perhaps burning or shredding it, as a sign of letting go? Will you keep it safely so as to reflect on it again in the future? Might you want to share it with a soul friend, or spiritual director?

# John the Baptiser

## Going out

Read Matthew 3:7–17.

This passage begins as quite a threatening passage, but goes on to promise a powerful baptism of Holy Spirit and fire, and to tell the story of Jesus' own baptism. It provides the template for this core Christian rite of passage, one which is accepted by the vast majority of churches throughout the world as the way of stepping over the threshold into becoming a Christian, and also often a member of a particular church. It's a great leveller, uniting all Christians, whatever their calling, whether they end as a bishop, or a sweeper up of glitter.

You may or may not have been baptised yourself, but I invite you to go out from your home and find some water—anything from a garden pond to the ocean. Ideally the water will be flowing, but if you can't find a river or stream, then still water is fine. Find a place to sit quietly within sight of the water.

If you have been baptised, remember the day of your baptism, or if you were baptised as a baby, imagine it. Who was there? Where did it take place? Was it your decision, and if so, what were your motives for taking this step?

If you haven't been baptised, reflect on what it would mean to take this step of faith. What draws you to it, and what prevents you from taking it?

Look at verses 16 and 17 where the Spirit of God descends on Jesus, and he hears the voice of God, confirming his identity. Have you ever experienced the presence of the Spirit of God, and had a sense of your calling as a Christian? Invite God to call you by name, to introduce you and express his feelings for you.

Before you return home, bend down, touch the water, and bless yourself with it, as a way of renewing your commitment to living out your identity as a beloved son or daughter of God.

# Jesus first and last

## Bible reading

Read Matthew 1:18–25.

How are the birth of Jesus and his passion linked? For much theology the answer is that God's first plan—recorded in the Old Testament, with the creation of Adam and Eve, their fall, God's calling of his people Israel, the kings and prophets—ultimately failed; and that Christ was sent primarily to put right the consequences of that failure and sin. If there had been no sin, there would have been no need for Christ to come.

But another theological tradition, and very much the Franciscan one, is that God always intended to share himself fully with the world he had created. The birth, life and death of Jesus were not an afterthought, or a plan B. Instead this tradition affirms that the cosmos without Christ would be incomplete, and therefore that the incarnation was always intended by God. This theology, developed by Bonaventure, an early Franciscan theologian, draws on the prologue to John's Gospel, and you might like to read John 1:1–14.

However, because sin had become a factor, this shaped the way in which the incarnation took place.

> Because of sin, we see the actual incarnation taking place in the mode of a suffering, crucified, and glorified Christ. That is, the incarnation takes place in such a way as to overcome the humanly constructed obstacles to achieving God's first aim: the sharing of divine life and love with creation.
>
> Zachary Hayes OFM, *The Gift of Being* (Liturgical Press, 2001), p. 105

If this is a new idea to you, how might it affect your journey through Lent? Consider how you personally hold together the beginning and the end of the life of Jesus, and how that life fits into God's greater picture.

## Temptation

### Imaginative

Read Matthew 4:1–11 at least twice, taking your time over it.

Today's invitation is to enter into this story and consider what it might teach you about temptation. The context is that Jesus has just been baptised and has had his identity confirmed. It's a crucial point in his life, and he goes off into the wilderness to fast for 40 days. He seems to have been considering how to live out his calling, and there were real choices to be made.

Sit comfortably; see the wilderness, with Jesus, hungry and tired from his fast. Do you know what makes you most open to temptation? It may be hunger or tiredness, or feeling alone or hurt.

The tempter comes, suggesting that Jesus can fulfil his need of food, can be exempt from the normal risks of life, and can have power beyond his imagining. What does 'the tempter' look like to you? And how does temptation work in your life?

The cost of each of the three things which the tempter offers Jesus is high. Go back to the story—what is the cost in each case? What are your particular temptations? We can use the idea lightly—of chocolate, shopping, or another drink—but try to look deeper. How are you tempted to misuse, or perhaps ignore, your God-given abilities, powers and gifts? And what is the cost of giving in to temptation?

Jesus each time answers with a verse of scripture (though notice that the devil is not above quoting scripture himself).

When you are tempted, what verses or stories from the Bible could you use to fight back?

Finish by praying that during this Lent you will recognise temptation when it comes, and learn how to resist it better.

## Called to serve

### Imaginative

Read Matthew 4:18–22.

John, son of Zebedee, remembers:

*I'm an old man now, and my memory isn't what it was. I can't preach any more, although people still come and ask me to speak to them. I just tell them, 'Love one another. That is the Lord's command and if you keep it, that by itself is enough.' Sometimes they look a bit disappointed—they hope for long stories of those years in Galilee and Jerusalem. But I've written the ones I want to pass on in my book.*

*Sometimes I have flashes of memory, vivid and bright, and it's as if it all happened yesterday. Leaving our father and his business—it was a huge thing to do, and yet it happened so quickly, and seemed inevitable. It wasn't the first time we'd met Jesus, of course. He was living in Capernaum, and we'd heard him preaching from time to time. There was something different about him, for sure. Not just his words, but how he was, how he looked at you. So when on this day he came along the shore, and we saw him stop and talk to Simon and Andrew, and then they left the nets and followed him—well, it was a shock, but...*

*Then they came to us, and Simon and Andrew were laughing and smiling at us, and Jesus just said, 'And how about you two?' and we found ourselves putting down our nets and tagging along. Our father was horrified, of course. But we couldn't do anything else. Perhaps that's something else I could tell those people who come to hear me? 'When he calls, answer. When he comes walking past, follow him.'*

# Blessed are you

## Liturgy

Read Matthew 5:1–12.

Use this prayer based on the passage as a way of making these strange blessings more personal. Changing from 'you' to 'I' may bring out the radical and countercultural nature of Jesus' words. If you find you can't with integrity say one or more of the lines, use that as a springboard to prayer for the ability to make that blessing your own, one day.

*Blessed am I when I know my need of God, for then God can rule in my life.*

**May it be so...**

*Blessed am I when I grieve, for grief opens up the way to God's comfort.*

**May it be so...**

*Blessed am I when I am content to be who I really am, not trying to be more important, for then I can live peacefully on the earth.*

**May it be so...**

*Blessed am I when my appetite is all for God and God's rule, for then I will never be hungry.*

**May it be so...**

*Blessed am I when I show mercy to others, for then my own need of mercy will be met.*

**May it be so...**

*Blessed am I when I keep my heart attuned to God, for then my eyes will see God in my life.*

**May it be so...**

*Blessed am I when I bring peace and forgiveness with me, for then I will be living as part of God's family.*

**May it be so...**

*Blessed am I when my faith brings me trouble, for then I am on the path to God's kingdom.*

**May it be so...**

## Piecing it together

### Creative

Go back over Matthew chapters 1—7. Are there any favourite passages missed out which you want to reflect on?

Recall what has struck you so far—what has been positive and helpful, what you have found difficult or puzzling. If you keep a journal, look back over your entries; sometimes even what seem great revelations disappear from the memory.

As a way of summing up your work with the start of Matthew's Gospel, make a collage. Take some magazines and leaf through them, looking for pictures, images, even simply colours which express something of your experience. They don't have to 'illustrate' particular ideas; let yourself simply be drawn to what catches your eye and your heart. Cut or tear out your chosen images and lay them on a table.

Then take a piece of card and begin to play with the images you have. How might they come together to make a collage which says something of your journey through these chapters? You don't have to use them all—some might not fit when you see them together.

Take your time, and do it reflectively and gently. When you feel ready, stick your collage together. You might want to date it on the back, and perhaps add a favourite verse to remind you of what inspired it.

Keep it somewhere you can see it regularly, and use it as a focus for your prayer through the rest of Lent. You may find you want to add to it during the rest of Lent.

# In the midst of the everyday: Matthew 8—12

*Lisa Cherrett*

## Come to me

### Introduction

These five chapters of Matthew's Gospel include some of the most well-loved and often-quoted words spoken by Jesus: 'Come to me, all you who are weary and burdened, and I will give you rest. Take my yoke upon you and learn from me, for I am gentle and humble in heart, and you will find rest for your souls. For my yoke is easy and my burden is light' (11:28–30, NIV).

I confess that I always imagine these comforting verses to be part of the Sermon on the Mount, which we read earlier in the Gospel. I feel that they fit better with Jesus' teaching on avoiding anxiety by contemplating the birds and flowers (6:25–34). It's very illuminating, therefore, to read the whole of Matthew 8—12, to see the context in which these words actually fit. From chapter 8 onward, when Jesus comes down from the mountain, there is a sense of constant movement and increasing hassle from all sides. He is always on the go, travelling from one place to another, crossing the lake, moving through towns and villages, meeting needy person after needy person.

We read in other places in the Gospels (for example, Mark 1:35) that Jesus sneaks away from the crowds to isolated places, to pray and renew his strength by spending time alone with his

Father God. In Matthew 8—12, though, there is no mention of him retreating from his ceaseless activity, no escape from the demanding crowds or the critical, muttering Pharisees. He takes no rest; he remains in the thick of the action, in the midst of conflict, doubt, challenge, dispute and harassment, facing the tyranny of religious rules and the deep ongoing needs of ordinary people.

Yet he promises to give us rest! We can only conclude that the words 'Come to me...' are not a command to retreat from the pressures of everyday life, with all its competing demands. Jesus is not beckoning us into quiet seclusion. Instead, he is inviting us to learn from him how to build a core of inner strength that enables us to find rest even in the midst of busyness, pressure and daily work.

Let's take a phrase at a time from Matthew 11:28–30, then, and see what we can learn from it.

## Come to Jesus

### Reflective

If we read through Matthew 8—12 (or, at least, look briefly at the beginning of each new section), it looks as if, when Jesus says 'Come to me...' (11:28), he is preaching to the converted. A remarkable number of different types of people, we're told, 'come' to Jesus with some sort of request. The leper, the centurion, the friends of the paralysed man, Jairus, the bleeding woman and two blind men come looking for healing, either for themselves or for others. A teacher of the law comes offering his services, tax collectors come to the party celebrating Matthew's joining of the disciples, and John the Baptist's disciples come (twice) to bring their puzzled questions and John's doubts about the way Jesus is conducting his ministry.

Stop and look back through this bewildering array of stories. We are being given a peek into the troubled hearts of many individuals here. Do you identify especially with any of them, or with any of the more passive onlookers who surround them? What would you say to Jesus if you were able to come to him, as these people did? What might he say to you? It took faith and courage for these characters to approach him, especially those—like the unclean leper and bleeding woman, the Gentile centurion and the 'sinful' tax collectors—who were not considered suitable recipients of any favours from a man of God, because they were on the margins of acceptable society.

Notice too, though, a group of people who are not described as 'coming' to Jesus. In 12:46–47, we are shown Jesus' mother and brothers 'standing outside'. These people who, we might think, deserve to be in the inner circle—his closest family—are pushed right to the edges of the milling crowd. 'Coming' to Jesus implies faith; at this point in the story, his family are not among those who come in faith.

Do you perhaps identify most strongly with them at this stage in your spiritual journey? Are you upset with Jesus because things haven't turned out the way you hoped or expected? Are you a bit indignant that Jesus seems to be paying more attention to newcomers to faith than he is to you?

If so, take heart! This is not the end of their story. By the time we get to Acts 1:14, his mother and brothers are on the inside, not the margins—meeting together with the core group of Jesus' disciples in the upper room, waiting for Pentecost.

# Weighed down

## Imaginative/creative

'Come to me, all you who are weary and burdened...' This is such an inclusive invitation. 'All you who are weary' must cover most people on earth. We are all weary of something, and the words certainly describe most of the people met by Jesus in these chapters. However, there were probably different causes for their weariness and feeling of being burdened.

Clearly the paralysed man brought to Jesus by his friends was burdened, whether he admitted it or not, by a sense of guilt. It was a secret burden until Jesus 'outed' it by proclaiming that his sins were forgiven. Matthew and his fellow tax collectors, too, must have been weary of being despised as collaborators with the Romans, lining their own pockets with the extra tax money that they extorted from their fellow Jews. To them, Jesus offered not condemnation but a dinner party.

How does it feel to be weary and burdened with a sense of guilt and sin? How does it feel to be given rest from that burden?

If you have a rucksack or a holdall, perhaps you could pack it full of objects that make it heavy—hardback books, tins or packets from the kitchen cupboard, or boots and shoes. Find some bulky items, fill your bag with them and then carry them around the house or garden for a while, feeling their weight pulling down your arms and bending your back.

As you walk, bring to God in prayer the weight of guilt that you might feel over particular words or actions. Have a time of confession and receive God's forgiveness and grace. Put down your bag, take the heavy objects out of it and feel the freedom of no longer having to carry that weight around. Thank God, in speech or song, for releasing you from your burdens.

# New for old

## Reflective/imaginative

Something else that can make us weary and burdened is the routine of life, the feeling that nothing exciting ever happens, or the weight of long-term responsibilities that seem unending. The 'same old same old' things we do every day can leave us needing refreshment. Traditions, whether church or family or personal traditions, can bring an unhelpful burden into our lives if we stick to them without really knowing why we do it.

Jesus believed and taught that his coming into the world would bring a radical change of focus, like a bridegroom arriving for his wedding to start a new and joyful married life (9:15). He taught that new beliefs can't be patched on to old ones, because the old is usually too inflexible to accommodate the new.

Are you feeling a strong call from God to branch out and do something completely new? Perhaps you have been a worship leader or a children's worker or a church flower arranger for a long time and people have come to rely on you to be there, filling that role. You feel the weight of other people's expectations and fear their surprise or disapproval if you were to step down—but God is inviting you into a new kind of service, which means that you will have to give up the old completely.

In prayer, imagine a shrunken old cloak next to a bright new roll of warm fabric, or an old tough leather wineskin and a glass of new, light, fresh wine. Lay these pictures out before God and ask, if you need to, for confirmation of his call and for courage to step out and embrace it.

If, as a result of your prayer, you realise that you are actually being called to stay a little longer in a role that has become mundane and unfulfilling, ask for courage to keep on working and waiting for the new opportunities that you seek to arrive at your door, in God's time, and that as you wait you may find fulfilment and enjoyment once more.

# Bearing others' burdens

## Intercession

Before we leave the idea of being weary and burdened, let's look away from ourselves and think for a while about the burdens that other people carry.

Turn the pages of a newspaper or go online to scroll through some news reports on the internet. You will very quickly find stories of people who are weary and burdened by various troubles of life, but look beyond the obvious examples and think, too, of the people you read about who seem to have everything they could wish for. There are particular burdens that come with fame and fortune; not everyone in the public eye wishes to be there, and news and opinion reports are often hurtful to the people they depict.

In the fast-paced world of online news reporting, where there is a clamour for new 'content' from hour to hour, even those who provide the news may become weary and burdened by the triviality or the cruelty of the stories they are expected to write.

Spend some time praying with compassion for one or two of the people whose predicaments catch your eye. Remember how inclusive Jesus' invitation is: 'Come to me, *all* who are weary and burdened.' Not everyone in the day's news may seem worthy of your prayers, but this is immaterial in the light of God's grace. There may be those who, you think, would never approach God with their own needs, but remember that some people who could not approach Jesus by themselves were brought to his attention by others who interceded for them.

# Rest for the weary

## Reflective

Now we move on to think about Jesus' words, '... and I will give you rest'. We've already noted how busy Jesus had been when he said these words. We might think that, given his own unceasing activity, he would say, 'Come to me... and I will give you even more challenges to face.' But no—he has *rest* to give, even in the midst of multiple demands on his time and energy.

Read again a few of the stories from Matthew 8—12 of Jesus' dealings with the needy people he met. He himself does not seem rushed or hassled. Jairus' demand for him to come and heal his dying daughter is an urgent one, but Jesus stops to pay full attention to the bleeding woman he meets on the way to Jairus' house. The disciples in the storm-ravaged boat are terrified and panicking, but Jesus is asleep. He is a centre, an oasis, of calm in a troubled environment. This is the kind of peace that he wants us to learn.

Perhaps this aura of peace and calm contributed to the sense of authority that there was about Jesus. This was the quality that marked him out as different from the usual religious teachers. His was a peace that made him stand out in a crowd, not fade into the background; that compelled people to listen when he spoke, not to ignore him.

Think of the people you know (or have known in the past). Do any of them have this kind of peaceful authority? What can you learn from observing them? Perhaps you yourself are one of those people. Has anyone said to you, 'You don't shout, but people really listen to you when you speak'? If so, ask God how you might develop this peaceful authority and use it in future to further his kingdom.

# The eye of the storm

## Creative

If you wanted to express peace in the midst of pressure and busyness in some kind of artistic form, how would you do it? It's said that the very centre of a tornado is a place of complete stillness. Use your imagination and try to produce a piece of artwork called 'In the eye of the storm' that you could display or perform. It might be a picture using paint, crayon or collage materials; a model made of clay, Plasticine or cardboard junk; a photograph, a sound recording, a dance or a poem. What colours, shapes or sounds would allow you to express most clearly the contrast between the storm and Jesus' peace?

Whatever you create, use it to aid your meditation on the 'rest' that Jesus promises, and let it lead you into restful prayer.

# Yoked with Jesus

## Going out/visual

When Jesus said, 'Take my yoke upon you and learn from me', again he wasn't talking about retreat from the everyday business of life. He was taking an image from the world of hard physical work—a pair of oxen pulling a plough—which would have been familiar to his first listeners. A young ox would be connected to an older one with a wooden bar laid across their shoulders, so that it would learn the steady, purposeful pace necessary to plough a straight furrow in a field.

The two animals would be trained to remain in step with each other. One couldn't race ahead or lag behind. They walked and worked together as equals. As they settled into that steady rhythm with one another, simply walking side by side, they could get a whole field ploughed without feeling the work as a pressure or a burden. Jesus said that this is how he wants us to learn from him: all our progress comes from being in step with him.

In today's Western culture, we have no first-hand experience of using yoked oxen but we have probably all seen or taken part in a three-legged race. If you have the chance, encourage some children you know (or some willing adults) to run a three-legged race outside. Show them how important it is to work together to establish a calm, relaxed, regular rhythm and to be in tune with each other's movements. The race winners will be the pair whose progress is the steadiest, not the most frantic.

Alternatively, find a partner and try ballroom dancing, or look on YouTube for a video you can watch. Again, see or feel how restful the dance can be when the partners are in step with each other, moving as one, rather than fighting each other or pulling in different directions.

Are you in step with Jesus, working with him rather than pulling against him?

## Looking back

### Reflective

Standing in a corner of a field at the beginning of the day's work, faced with a cumbersome wooden plough and a pair of uncommunicative oxen, a ploughman could be forgiven for feeling a little daunted at the task ahead. However, for the oxen themselves, simply putting one foot in front of another and settling into that steady shared rhythm meant that they would cover a lot of ground without feeling the strain. At the end of the day, the job would be done.

When I was a child, the road home from school and the town centre shops was slightly uphill, in a long, straight line, and my mother didn't drive. Our house wasn't visible from the main road, and the walk seemed to take for ever. One of my coping strategies for this regular ordeal was to set my eyes on a goal just ahead—say, the next lamp-post—reach it, and then look back to see how far I'd come. Looking at the stretch of pavement in front of me was depressing; looking back at the ground I'd covered, getting longer with every pause, was more helpful.

It's encouraging to stand still, from time to time, and look back to see how far we've come in our Christian life. If you have a spiritual journal or a book in which you record your prayers, take a short while to turn back the pages and remind yourself of where you were standing, spiritually, months or years earlier. Can you find prayers that have been answered, bad habits that have been broken, difficult relationships that have become happier, or new ministries that have blossomed—all because you have walked in step with Jesus?

What are the issues and concerns that you face now? Can you look ahead with more confidence, seeing how far you've already come?

# Meekness

## Reflective

'Learn from me, for I am gentle and humble in heart,' said Jesus. Meditate for a while on the way Jesus describes himself here. It's amazing enough to think that the almighty and eternal God should come to earth as a human being, brought up as the son of a local carpenter/builder, and then, in his public ministry, wander among the towns and villages of the unexciting region of Galilee with 'nowhere to lay his head' (8:20). How much more astonishing it is, though, that he should compare himself in these verses to a common farm animal, trudging through acres of mud to prepare a field for the growing of basic foodstuffs. Elsewhere in the Bible, Jesus is described as the majestic Lion of Judah (Revelation 5:5), but here he is a working beast of burden.

Not only that, but he offers himself to us as a teacher who walks through the mud with us, side by side in close and intimate partnership. There is another relationship to consider, too. A pair of oxen does not work independently; it is put to work by a farmer. Elsewhere in the Gospels, Jesus says that he himself does not work alone but does 'only what he sees his Father doing' (John 5:19). 'I am the true vine,' he says, 'and my Father is the gardener' (John 15:1). We might say that in Matthew 11 Jesus is the experienced ox but his Father is the ploughman. Like the centurion in chapter 8, Jesus is 'a man under authority, with soldiers under me'.

Yet another point not to be missed is that the ox is a powerful beast: we use the comparison 'as strong as an ox' to describe a weightlifter or bodybuilder. Strength under control, under authority, is the definition of 'meekness'—and only a few chapters earlier in Matthew's Gospel, Jesus has said, 'Blessed are the meek, for they will inherit the earth' (5:5).

## How Would Jesus Do It?

### Creative

If we are followers of Jesus, we too need to be 'gentle and humble in heart', at rest even in the midst of pressure. The phrase 'What Would Jesus Do?' is very well known as a way of reminding Christians of the need to become more and more like him as we make decisions in everyday life. You might have seen wristbands bearing the letters WWJD?

However, this often seems too difficult a question to answer when we try to apply it to situations that Jesus never encountered because he didn't live in our technologically advanced society. I'm not sure anyone can satisfactorily answer the question 'What type of car would Jesus drive?' or 'Would Jesus be on Facebook?' It may be profitable to think instead in terms of the character qualities he displayed. Matthew quotes Isaiah 42 to give a further illustration of Jesus' gentleness: 'A bruised reed he will not break, and a smouldering wick he will not snuff out' (Matthew 12:20). This is a picture of someone who is careful with fragile people—not walking on eggshells around difficult neighbours but taking positive steps to protect and encourage those who need support.

There are other qualities as well. In chapter 10, Jesus tells his disciples to be bold, shrewd and fearless in their witness to him. We might also think of his quick wit in answering his critics, his authority, his imaginative and creative language, and his compassion and generosity towards people everywhere. All these aspects of Jesus' character are evident in Matthew 8—12.

How can we develop those characteristics when we are driving a car of any type, whenever we're posting on Facebook or other internet forums, when we are queuing at the shops or when we answer the phone to a cold caller? Perhaps the question to ask might be not 'What Would Jesus Do?' but 'How Would Jesus Do It?'

Could you make a wristband or a card to carry in your pocket, with the letters HWJDI on it? (Craft shops sell small beads with letters of the alphabet on them.) When faced with a decision about what action might be most Christ-like in a given situation, your HWJDI band might help to remind you of Jesus' words, 'Learn from me, for I am gentle and humble in heart.'

# Come to him for inner strength

## Prayer

As we finish our reflections on Matthew 11:28–30 and the surrounding chapters, you might like to bring your thoughts together in a prayer:

*Thank you, Lord Jesus, that I can come to you at any time and in any place, whether I'm feeling happy and confident or weary and burdened.*
*I come to you again, now with these issues on my mind… [name them to God].*
*I come to you in faith; please grant my requests.*
*I come to you in doubt; please meet me in my questioning.*
*I come to you in courage; send me out with boldness to speak of your kingdom.*
*I come to you in fear; reassure me of your presence, and release me from all anxiety.*
*I bring to you my daily work; walk beside me in it, and help me to learn your steady and purposeful rhythm of life.*
*I bring to you the people who rely on me for support; help me to heal the bruised reed and fan into flame the smouldering wick.*
*Thank you for the rest you offer, and the strength you give. Amen*

# The kingdom: Matthew 13—22

*Sally Welch*

## 'Listen!': hearing the word of the kingdom

### Bible reading

Read Matthew 13:1–12.

On my daily walks into the countryside I notice the activity and sheer hard work that goes into caring for my surroundings. I see the way the fields are ploughed, fertilised and sown with mechanical seed drills ensuring that not one seed is wasted. How unlike these careful stewards of the earth is the farmer in this parable! His work is many times harder, as he has to cast each precious seed by hand. Yet Jesus tells us that the seed is scattered not just in the best places, but also in the most hostile of territory. What sort of farmer wastes his most precious commodity in this way? To demonstrate further that this story goes against our expectations, this same improvident farmer is blessed with the most astounding harvest!

The news of God's kingdom, news which it is our privilege to know and to share, is not to be guarded and protected, shared only with those whom we consider most worthy to accept it. Instead it is to be shared joyfully, generously, profligately, with everyone we meet, whether they seem likely to take it on board or not. None of us is worthy to receive God's word, but nevertheless we are all offered it, for with God as the farmer, who knows what sort of crops it will raise?

Next time you go for a walk, whether it is in the countryside, in a park or simply down your street, look for plants growing in unlikely places. See how they cling to stones, or force their way up through cracks in the pavements, springing up in the smallest amount of soil. So too will news of God's kingdom find its way into the darkest spaces, filling them with light and hope. We must not be afraid to share this news even in the unlikeliest places; we never know who might be listening!

# Tiny seeds

## Creative

Read Matthew 13:31–32.

This tiny parable, only a few verses long, has always captured my imagination. Remembering the frail, single-stemmed plant that I used to grow on a flannel on the windowsill when I was a child, I could not imagine how such a fragile thing could grow so large, much less support a bird! But the mustard tree of biblical times was far from being merely a grassy sandwich filling. Scholars believe that the parable refers to black mustard (*Brassica nigra*), a large plant, usually considered as a shrub. Wild mustard plants still grow near the Jordan River and they can grow to over 10 feet tall, large and bushy, with many small green leaves and tiny yellow flowers. As the plant grows, its stem becomes large and woody, making it look more like a tree. By mid-summer, when the shrub is at its fullest, a strong mustard tree will provide cool shade in which birds can shelter from the hot sun.

Although the seeds of this tree were not the smallest the listeners would have seen, it is the rapid growth from such a tiny beginning that is the wonderful thing. So too, says Jesus, is the growth of the kingdom, when those who hear God's words act on them. Why not buy a packet of mustard and cress seeds and sprinkle them on a damp paper towel on your windowsill? Keep the towel damp and within a few days the seeds will sprout. As you watch the seeds grow, consider how your words and actions 'take root' and affect your life and the lives of those around you. Loving gestures, kind words, generous acts, however small they seem, bring the kingdom daily closer. Take care also to notice the small signs of love that surround you, the possibilities of God reaching into our world—notice them, give thanks for them, and share them with others.

# Hidden treasures

## Meditative

Read Matthew 13:44–46.

Hidden deep in the soil, in the damp darkness, lies the incredible treasure. For the moment it is known only to the animals and insects that live underground, the worms that slide past, the beetles that carve tiny tunnels, hitting the solid edges of the box in which the treasure is buried and moving away at a tangent to find a softer place to burrow. Only the dedicated seeker, digging deep into the ground, turning over the soil, alert and watchful—only they will find the silent riches. Even then, the seeker must sacrifice everything else they have before it will finally be in their possession.

The pearl does not lie buried in the ground; it is hidden in the open, on the market stall, in the bazaar, rolling large and luminescent among other, lesser pearls, whose humble appearance masks the lustre of this single, perfect specimen. The diligent merchant, sharp-eyed, spots this wondrous object and pays the price that is demanded, though it is great indeed. But they are happy to pay, for to own this pearl is their sole desire.

The kingdom of heaven is to be found among the everyday

activities and objects of our lives. It is to be seen in our daily interactions with family, friends and neighbours. It is to be caught up in the glimpses of the glory of God's creation that surrounds us. It asks great things of us—patience, loving kindness, forgiveness—but will give back the same to us in even greater abundance.

But first we must actively seek it, not be put off by the dirt or the dust, nor distracted by the tawdry glitter of fake promises, but prepared to sacrifice much to find it. And once we have found it, never to let go.

Where will you seek the kingdom of heaven today? In whom will you find it? How will you share your knowledge of it?

## Things new… and old

### Creative

Read Matthew 13:52.

I was fortunate enough last year to be invited to join a group who were going on a retreat by the Sea of Galilee. The first afternoon of my arrival, even before I had unpacked, I hurried down to the shoreline. Here was the lake I had read about, preached on, imagined. I allowed the gentle waves to lap at my toes. Taking out my phone, I photographed my feet, covered in the sparkling waters of that familiar, yet unknown, place. Now, when I feel in need of peace, or support, or simply to remind myself what it is all about, I scroll to that photo and give thanks.

Make yourself a 'treasure chest'. It can be a physical box, a photograph album, or a set of pictures on your phone, put in a separate album, away from the rest of your photos. Into this treasure chest, put objects or photographs of people, landscapes and things that mean a lot to you. They can be anything you like—you do not have to justify to anyone else what you include.

All that these objects or pictures need to do is to be reminders of some of the blessings you have experienced in your life. Do not be afraid to include photos of people you loved who are now dead, or of places which were dear to you in the past—the passage tells us to include things 'old and familiar' among our treasures. Do try to put in those things or people in which you rejoice nowadays—things 'new and fresh'. In this way, the unbroken line of God's promises to you will stretch back to your birth and on into your future, whatever that may bring.

Take time to pray with and for those people and places in your treasure box, signs of the kingdom breaking through and filling our lives with joy and love.

# Costly grace

## Spotlight

Read Matthew 16:25–28.

Dietrich Bonhoeffer was born in 1906 in Breslau, now Wroclaw in Poland, to a happy settled academic family. He read theology at Tübingen University and then went to Berlin to continue his studies. He studied in America before returning to teach at Berlin. He was ordained priest at the age of 25 and seemed set for an illustrious academic career. All this was abandoned when Hitler came to power, as Bonhoeffer campaigned from the outset against the persecution of the Jews. He travelled to London in 1933 but returned to Germany in 1935, devoting himself to opposing Nazism. In 1943 he was arrested by the Gestapo for his involvement in the plot to kill Hitler. In prison, and later in Flossenburg concentration camp, he inspired all with his courage, his unselfishness and his goodness—even to his guards. His concern was to get permission to minister to the sick and his fellow prisoners. All who met him were impressed by his calm and his self-control. Three weeks before Adolf Hitler killed himself, he ordered the execution of Bonhoeffer.

Throughout his life and imprisonment, to the moment of his death, Bonhoeffer preached and wrote—and lived as he preached. He contrasted the 'cheap grace' which was 'grace without discipleship, grace without the cross', with the 'costly grace' which calls all people to follow Christ: 'it is costly because it costs a man his life, and it is grace because it gives a man the only true life' (*The Cost of Discipleship*, 1937).

As we explore what it means to seek God's kingdom, we must be ever mindful of the cost that we must pay. Let us pray for the courage and the determination to follow Christ, with Peter, wherever he might lead us.

> The cross is not a terrible end to an otherwise God-fearing and happy life, but it meets us at the beginning of our communion with Christ, for it is Christ whom the disciple finds as he picks up his cross.
>
> *The Cost of Discipleship*, 1937

## Who is the greatest?

### Meditative

Read Matthew 18:1–6.

Who knows how the argument started? The disciples had been on the road with Jesus for a while and it seemed as if they would never stop; the teachings, the healings, the miracles. Strange and wonderful times, but perplexing and exhausting. Added to this was the constant necessity to arrange food and accommodation, to give Jesus time to rest and recover—who was going to be in charge of all that? Perhaps they fought for the privilege of caring for Jesus; perhaps they fought over who was to be the unofficial servant among them. So, when tempers flared and the dispute grew too heated, they took it to Jesus: 'Who is the greatest?'

As usual Jesus, as a true and loving teacher, helps the disciples to find their own answer. A small child serves to illustrate the message; a person of importance in that the child will help to preserve the line of David, but in itself, of no interest or value—or so the disciples think. But no, for Jesus declares that this insignificant being, vulnerable and helpless, is more important than they are. What a bitter blow to their pride! What a shock to their world view!

The kingdom of heaven, Jesus says, is not about how rich you are, or how powerful, or where your family comes from. It is about how you treat those who are weaker than you. The child standing in the middle of the circle of angry, aggressive adults is a living reminder of the effect our actions can have upon those around us, helpless in the face of conflicts and wrath.

How do we behave among people we consider to be our inferior, whether in wealth, intelligence or power? How do we treat those who serve us in cafés and bars, those who provide services for us? What do we say to the elderly and the very young in our community to show they are valued and cherished by kingdom seekers?

## Where two or three are gathered in my name

### Prayer

Read Matthew 18:19–20.

Use these prayers to join with others as you pray:

O God, early in the morning I cry to you. Help me to pray and to concentrate my thoughts on you: I cannot do this alone. In me there is darkness, but with you there is light; I am lonely, but you do not leave me; I am feeble in heart, but with you there is help; I am restless, but with you there is peace.

In me there is bitterness, but with you there is patience; I do not understand your ways, but you know the way for me... Restore me to liberty, and enable me so to live now that I may answer before you and before me. Lord, whatever this day may bring, your name be praised.

Dietrich Bonhoeffer

Lord, come to me; my door is open.

Michel Quoist, 1918–97

Work thy holy will in me and through me this day. Protect me, guide me, bless me, within and without, that I may do something this day for love of thee.

Edward Bouverie Pusey, 1800–82

Grant us to look with your eyes of compassion, O merciful God, at the long travail of mankind: the wars, the hungry millions, the natural disasters, the cruel and needless deaths, men's inhumanity to one another, the heartbreak and hopelessness of so many lives. Hasten the coming of the messianic age when the nations shall be at peace, and men shall live free from fear and free from want and there shall be no more pain or tears, in the security of your will, the assurance of your love, the coming of your kingdom, O God of righteousness, O Lord of compassion.

George Appleton, 1902–93

# What must I do?

## Bible reading

Read Matthew 19:16–26.

This story begins like so many others—a man in desperate need comes up to Jesus and asks for healing. But, unlike the blind and the maimed, the possessed and the leprous, this man rejects the healing that he has asked for, as the price is too high.

It seems as if he has everything he needs—in fact, this young man is so well satisfied with the things of this life that he can afford to seek the things of the next. His is not a life of quiet desperation, trapped by physical or mental ill health, and he believes he is in a good position to chase after the next desirable achievement. Accustomed to paying for what he wants, to instant gratification, he is sure this wish of his will be gratified. But although his illness is not outwardly grave, it is in fact the most desperate of all. The man is sick with wealth, possessed by his possessions. Jesus offers him healing, but the man cannot allow himself to be freed, choosing instead to remain trapped in a prison of his own making.

If we have all we need, we can believe we are self-sufficient. If money can buy most things, we can believe it will buy everything. What we have becomes who we are. Life itself becomes a commodity, not a gift.

The kingdom of heaven is free to those who are free to enter it. What must I do to inherit eternal life? I must let go of everything that gets in the way, and let go of believing that I can save myself, for only God can save me.

What are the things that get in the way of our trust in God? How can we sit lightly to the things of this world—material possessions, good health, personal influence—so that we may leave them behind to enter the next?

# It's not fair!

## Bible reading

Read Matthew 20:1–16.

There is a famous psychology experiment in which a group of young children are each given a gift. Most of the children receive the same item—something fun and good quality. A few don't receive anything, just an empty box, and their reactions are then studied. Some respond with anger, some with despair; some complain to the nearest adults; others, who have already learnt life's bitter lessons, accept with resignation. A few wait hopefully, sure that this injustice will be corrected.

Our reaction to this passage can be like that of children—how can it be fair that those who have not worked nearly as long or as hard can be given the same reward?

The parable seems to fly in the face of all that we learn about the fairness and justice of God's kingdom. But we need to consider that those who were employed to work at the beginning of the day passed the time in a productive, profitable way. Like the happy children in the experiment, they did not have to worry whether they would receive anything; they were secure. Those who were left in the playground without a toy, in the market square without a job, had an anxious, miserable time before they received their reward.

More importantly still, let us be assured that none of us deserves to enter into the kingdom of heaven. That we do so at all is by God's grace alone; to quibble about the entry qualifications of others is foolish in the face of our patent unworthiness. God reaches out to us and to others in great love. We can respond to that love by sharing it with others, beginning with small acts of unobtrusive kindness, offered to neighbour and colleague, liked or not liked. So we will help to build up the kingdom that is founded not only on the principle of fairness, but on the fact of boundless love and mercy.

# Donkey work

## Meditative

Read Matthew 21:1–7.

You could say one thing for life with Jesus: it was never dull! The disciples could never truly understand why they had done it, why they had dropped everything and gone with him, but they were glad they had. They had seen wonderful sights, witnessed miraculous healings, heard powerful stories, all in the company of that quiet man who held so much love within him. They had enjoyed the status of being disciples of Jesus, revelling in the reflected glory of the man that everyone wanted to meet. They had argued over which of them was the most important, who was doing the best job and so deserved the greatest reward, but Jesus had put them firmly in their place—the task of the leader is to serve the people, not exploit the power.

So they continued with the everyday chores of finding meals and accommodation—and now this. A donkey must be found, one with a foal, stable owners negotiated with and the two truculent animals, torn from their regular routine, wrestled along the path back to Jesus. Where was the glamour now? It had fallen in the dung and straw of the stable. What confidence was this, so secure in his place in the eternal realm that the power of this world held no attractions for him! The disciples could but dimly glimpse the glory behind the everyday, the kingdom in the acts of service, but they could trust their Master and so they struggled with the reluctant beasts, unknowingly playing their part in the prophecy of the King, the Messiah, the Chosen One.

We do not know the details of God's plans for us, but we can pray humbly for the grace to carry out the tasks allotted to us, confident that they have a place bringing the kingdom of heaven to earth.

*Teach me, my God and King,*
*In all things thee to see,*
*And what I do in anything,*
*To do it as for thee.*

George Herbert

## The cornerstone

### Creative

Read Matthew 21:33–44.

Over a lifetime of prayer and intercession, we may make many requests of God. In some cases, our requests will be answered in a straightforward and simple way. At other times we may discover, through prayer, that those things which we believed would be best for us or for those on our hearts might not be the right solution after all. There are prayers which we offer year after year and for which we are still awaiting an answer; these can be challenging. Occasionally, and joyfully, our prayers may be answered in ways which we could never have imagined but which turn out to be the most wonderful solution.

All these different answers to prayer have one thing in common—we tend to forget about them! As soon as the need is met, or the situation has changed, we move on and bring a new set of issues and problems before God.

Find a large surface for your prayers. If you cannot find a permanent place, such as a stretch of wall or a table, small noticeboards can be bought very cheaply and covered in bright wrapping paper to make them attractive. A large piece of card or paper would do the job, but take care that it does not get too scruffy.

At the bottom of your board write or print: 'The Lord has done this and it is marvellous in our eyes' (Matthew 21:42). Then, using post-it notes, cards or simply writing onto your paper, write down your intercessions as you pray them. Continue to do this over a number of days and weeks, and each time the situation about which you prayed changes, note this also. Do not remove the answered prayers; leave them as a record of God's love and grace.

At the end of each month, look back over the prayers which have been answered, and thank God for all that he has done. Use your answered prayers to help you journey forward in your prayer life.

# The wedding banquet is ready

## Bible reading

Read Matthew 22:1–14.

Marriage in New Testament times was a civil rather than a religious affair. Betrothal would occur at an early age, a contract being made which was as binding as a marriage. The bridegroom would then spend about a year preparing a home, often an extension to his father's house, while the bride gathered her trousseau and prepared for married life. When the bridegroom was ready to receive the bride, he would go to her family home, where she would be waiting, dressed in her wedding finery. The simple marriage ceremony would take place there, followed by a feast at the home of the groom or, as in this case, the groom's parents. This feast would be an opportunity to demonstrate the wealth and hospitality of the bridegroom's family and could last many days.

Jesus compares the kingdom of heaven to the hospitality of a rich man who has spent much time and money preparing a feast for his beloved son. Annoyed that those who should have accepted his hospitality turn it down, he opens the invitation to everyone in the neighbourhood, the only proviso being their readiness to join in the celebrations.

Are we ready to accept our invitation to the heavenly banquet, or have we let material concerns and preoccupations get in our way? Are we willing to spend time and effort in getting ready, or do we expect simply to enter the kingdom of heaven unprepared?

The kingdom of heaven is as beautiful as a pearl and as valuable as treasure. It can grow from tiny beginnings within us into something precious and useful, but we have to be prepared to enter it. We have actively to seek the kingdom, not allowing anything to obscure our search, but we will be helped on our quest by the One who came to open the doors of the kingdom for us, and who will guide us there, if we but ask.

# Formed by the word of God: Matthew 23—28

*Jean Marie Dwyer OP*

## Formed by the word of God

### Introduction

The word of God needs to be the foundation of our spiritual life. Studying, reading and praying with the scripture allows God's word to enter into our heart and inserts our daily living into God's plan. We continue our journey with the Gospel of Matthew using chapters 23—28, which cover the end of Jesus' ministry, his death and resurrection and the commissioning of the apostles. The texts are powerfully formative of our faith. Our prayerful interaction with Matthew's texts will lead to a greater understanding of discipleship. We will grapple with the meaning of the texts as a way of becoming a better follower of Christ. Our purpose is to read Matthew with new eyes and to be followers not only in word but in our daily living and in truth.

We also want to use these texts as a preparation for walking with Jesus in his passion, death and resurrection. As Jesus entered into our pain and sorrow, so may our study of this section of the Gospel help us to an ever deeper understanding of God's great gift in sending his Son for our salvation.

# The gospel and integrity of life

## Intercession/imaginative

Read Matthew 23:1–12.

Jesus' message to the crowd and to his disciples was of integrity of life. He denounces the scribes and Pharisees for teaching one thing and living another. Jesus acknowledges their position of authority and the validity of their teaching but not their example. For our life to be integral there must be a cohesion between our inner heart and our actions. Merely to speak or teach ideals without the lived reality in our life is a lie. Jesus condemns the Pharisees for showing off, wanting to appear good rather than really to be good. Jesus calls them hypocrites. They are not what they seem (23:5–9).

Our love for one another is the only standard for judging our love for God. Matthew's teaching here (23:4–12) impacts how we love. True love for our neighbour is the gift of self in loving service. Jesus also condemns the scribes and Pharisees for exalting themselves, seeking the best places, wanting to be important. Doing these things makes our love for others less because we put ourselves in a superior position and look down upon them.

Read Matthew 23:1–12 slowly.

As you read, think about the following:

Do you ask or expect from others what you are not doing or willing to do?

Could you take time to compliment one of your co-workers or to help someone in the workplace or at home to accomplish a task they struggle with?

Choose one particular point from this section of the Gospel to work on so that it becomes a part of your daily living.

Think of someone you know who irritates you.

How does he or she irritate you?

What in their actions do you find unpleasant?
Do they do things that are morally wrong, or just insensitive?
How would you change them and why?
Now imagine Jesus standing beside this person with his hand on their shoulder.
Enter into silent prayer with Jesus. Ask Jesus how he sees this person.
Continue to pray for this person every day for the next week.

# Blind guides

## Reflective

Read Matthew 23:13–29.

In this section of the Gospel Jesus levels strong accusations against the Pharisees and scribes. They are blind guides because they are not willing to see their neighbours with love. Their unwillingness to help their neighbour by the gift of loving service is met with severe criticism from Jesus. We need to take seriously Jesus' criticism and allow this message to have a transforming effect on our lives.

Read slowly and meditatively the 'woes' sections of Matthew 23:13–29.

Journal about why Jesus condemns their actions and what remedy he recommends. Apply this to your life.

# The divine mercy

## Bible study

Read Matthew 23:37–39.

Jesus' lament over Jerusalem reflects God's loving mercy and steadfast love for his people. Throughout the Old Testament and in Jesus' teaching we are constantly assured of God's love and forgiveness if we open our hearts to receive it.

Do a word search of 'steadfast love' through the entire Bible. It is a very important phrase to become familiar with, related to the covenant. Write down some of the ways the phrase is used for God's love. Receive that steadfast love. How do you want to respond? Make a practical list to work on.

(The website www.biblegateway.com would be a helpful study tool for this exercise.)

# The coming of the Son of Man

## Bible study

Read Matthew 24:3–35.

There are many important themes for our faith in chapter 24 of Matthew's Gospel. Jesus' disciples are very curious about the signs of the end of time (see, for example, vv. 3–28). People today still want to know when Jesus is coming again and many have falsely predicted the day. Jesus was very clear that only the Father knows the time. Many of the signs named in the text we have with us in each new generation.

Divide the chapter into sections and spend time studying the teaching of each section:

- 24:3–28 Jesus on the Mount of Olives
- 24:29–31 The coming of the Son of Man
- 24:32–35 The lesson of the fig tree

Write down important words that can help to transform your life. What important messages does each section contain for growing in holiness? Are there 'hard sayings'? How do they help us to focus on seeking holiness of life?

## The necessity for watchfulness

### Reflective/creative

Read Matthew 24:36–51.

Jesus exhorts us on the importance of being ready because we do not know the time of God's coming. We need to be prepared. We have the examples of Noah and watching for a thief in the night. Stay awake and watch. The Son of Man is coming at an unexpected hour.

Read Matthew 24:36–44 and apply this reading to daily preparedness for the times God will visit you during this day. The best way to prepare for Jesus' coming in glory is by living each day in God's presence, seeking to do his will.

Be very alert today for the times God will visit you with his grace in unexpected ways, perhaps in the guise of someone difficult to work with or by humbly accepting someone's suggestion of a way in which you can improve.

Be ready for the unexpected challenges to live virtuously.

Make a list of five things that will help you to live in a more God-centred way. Work on that list and put it into practice.

Read Matthew 24:45–51.

How do you answer Jesus' question on who is the faithful servant? What does it mean to be faithful? How far are you willing to go in order to be a faithful disciple?

## Parables of waiting

### Creative

Read Matthew 25:1–46.

Jesus tells us in the Gospel that we will not know the day or hour of his coming. We need always to be prepared. Holiness of life prepares us for the kingdom. If, in our daily living, we are seeking to follow Jesus, then the time of his coming in glory need not worry us. In this section of Matthew's Gospel there are several parables on waiting alertly for the coming of the Lord. We have the parable of the ten bridesmaids, the parable of the talents, and the judgement of the nations.

## The parable of the ten bridesmaids (25:1–13)

Why is Jesus telling this story? Matthew is primarily addressing the Jews. In its context the message is first for Matthew's audience. Only after understanding the meaning in its context do we move to what the text is saying to us in our circumstances. Look at the texts that came before this story. The whole chapter is the context for understanding this parable.

In your own words retell the story of the ten bridesmaids. Put it into modern language. Tell a modern parable, perhaps with other characters, but remain faithful to Jesus' original storyline. Be creative. Use this approach for all three parables.

## The parable of the talents (25:14–30)

One of the important considerations of this story is the power that fear can have over us. Our fears can prevent us from experiencing the joy of following Jesus and freely serving others.

Reflect on the fears that hold you back from living life fully and freely.

Give special attention to verse 29, 'For to all those who have, more will be given, and they will have an abundance; but from those who have nothing, even what they have will be taken away' (NRSV).

### The judgement of the nations (25:31–46)

This section also has the beautiful teaching on the judgement of the nations. Jesus will not condemn us. Our relationship to our neighbour is the criterion for the final judgement. We judge ourselves by the way we have lived our life.

Matthew 25:31–46 is such a familiar passage, but read it with new eyes. Read and pray over it in order to apply it to your relationships in a very concrete way. How can this word change your daily choices and the way you are present to others—those you love but also the stranger, the poor, the marginalised? At his coming Jesus will ask us how we loved.

Begin a daily habit of reaching out in love to at least one person.

# Jesus' condemnation

## Imaginative

Read Matthew 26:1–16.

After Jesus tells the disciples about love as the criterion for our judgement at the end of time, he tells them that he will be crucified. This is such a stark contrast and too much for his followers. Jesus' words do not fit their expectations of the Messiah. The drama takes on a new dimension as the chief priests and elders meet to arrest Jesus secretly and have him killed. In these verses we have three sets of characters and dialogues: the gathering of the chief priests and the elders with Caiaphas, Jesus at the house of Simon, and Judas' offer to betray Jesus.

Read, study and pray with each one of these sections separately.

Take note of each character and listen carefully to the

dialogue: small details are often important for understanding the richness and full import of Matthew's message.

## The chief priests and elders (vv. 3–5)

As you study and pray with the text, imagine yourself present with the chief priests and elders. Listen to their dialogue and enter into it. From the Gospel of John we know that not all the elders agreed: think of Nathanael and Joseph of Arimathea who sympathised with Jesus.

What do you think they are feeling?
What is motivating their actions?
What can you learn from their actions?
Write down your insights and apply them to your life.

## Jesus at Bethany (vv. 6–13)

There is certainly a lot going on in this story; strong emotions are expressed. A very small detail speaks volumes about Jesus and his ministry. In verse 6 we are told that Jesus is staying in the house of Simon the leper. All the Gospels emphasise that Jesus embraces those who are shunned and isolated.

Compare the text of Matthew with that of Luke (7:36–50) and John (12:1–8).

## Judas' betrayal (vv. 14–16)

In just three verses we are told that Judas sold Jesus for 30 pieces of silver and from that moment began to look for a way to betray him. He lived with Jesus and travelled with him, saw his kindness and his miracles. For so little he eagerly waited for a way to betray him. Such a sad text. What went wrong?

Sit in the presence of this text and pray with it—perhaps in a church or sacred spot. What do you learn from it for your own life? Be with Judas; pray about what he is doing. What brought him to this? Pray with him. Try to understand his weakness. What is hard for you in interacting with Judas?

Continue to reflect on this scene of the betrayal and arrest of Jesus from Matthew 26:47–56.

Judas betrays Jesus like a friend, with a kiss.

Read the text very slowly and, as the story unfolds, pause and reflect on the dynamism of the actions. Compare Jesus' demeanour to that of his disciples. The crowd is violent. Jesus' disciples use a show of power. Jesus knows everything is in his Father's hands.

How often do we respond to impossible situations with violence and anger? We need to be in control and yet there is so much in life we have no control over. How can we deepen our faith in the power of God in our life?

Continue to pray with the text in the light of the above questions. Add other questions that come to mind. Journal about how this text affects you and how it gives you wisdom to be transformed. Everything in the word of God is spoken for our healing and transformation.

## Events preparing for Jesus' death

### Maundy Thursday

Read Matthew 26:17–28.

Every year we celebrate the three great days of Holy Week that commemorate Jesus' last days on earth. They begin with the institution of the Lord's Supper which is commemorated on Holy Thursday. Jesus prepares for his death by gathering with his disciples to celebrate the Passover, a yearly holy day of remembrance for the Jews of God's deliverance of his people from Egypt. Then comes Good Friday, which commemorates the crucifixion and death of Jesus. Holy Saturday is the day Jesus was laid in the tomb. In the early Church this was a day of silence, prayer, waiting and expectation.

If you can, gather as a family or with friends and read together Exodus 12:1–20. Share together the meaning of this text. What might it have meant to Israel? God is faithful to his people. Talk about how it prefigures Christ. What does it mean to you today?

Read together Matthew's account of the Lord's Supper (vv. 26–29). Offer a prayer of thanksgiving and praise.

Or you could attend a Holy Thursday service. Try living the whole day in thanksgiving.

Jesus leaves the Passover meal and enters into his suffering.

Read the next three events in the Holy Week narrative, and then answer the three questions about the events:

- Jesus prays in Gethsemane (26:36–46)
- Jesus before the high priest (26:57–68)
- Peter's denial of Jesus (26:69–75)

What do the events mean to you?
What has Jesus done for you?
What is your response?

## The way of the cross

### Good Friday

Read Matthew 27:1–26.

In this section we accompany Jesus as he makes his way to the cross, the sign of God's love and our salvation. Jesus freely lays down his life for us. It is in these passages we see him bearing the full brunt of our human weakness and sin.

Choose a quiet spot to read the text slowly. Visualise the scene and become one of the characters—a witness to what is taking place. First write out the scene as you imagine it. Then through silent prayer be present to the scene as you have written it.

Take note of the various characters involved and the dynamic between them. Ponder deeply Jesus' presence in each scene, his words and actions. Try to become one with his sentiments and sorrow.

*As Pilate's secretary I take notes of what is happening. I stand beside Pilate so I have a good view of the so-called king of the Jews. He stands there with dignity, a man with such a gentle, patient face, etched with infinite sorrow. Who is this man? There is something so different, even special, about him. My master begins to question him.*

*'Are you a king?'*

*Jesus answers quietly and somehow with a hidden power that is strange to behold. Doesn't he understand Pilate's power to condemn him? I think my master also feels the strange mystery about this man. When the chief priests and elders accuse him, he makes no answer, just looks at them with such pity. I have heard that he has tried many times to help them understand but to no avail. So now his only answer can be silence—all has been said. Pilate is amazed at his silence, that he does not defend himself. I feel so touched by this silent man with his gentleness and the power that lies within him. Even in his bonds he seems like a king.*

# The death and burial of Jesus

## Holy Saturday

Read Matthew 27:32–66.

When Jesus dies, a great darkness comes over the whole land. How forlorn the followers of Jesus must have been. Hope was dead. All their plans and visions of a new world had been shattered. What feelings of confusion filled their grieving hearts? Their Messiah was dead.

Divide this passage into sections and read slowly, noticing what is happening: the events of the way of the cross, Jesus' crucifixion, his death and burial. You may like to record your thoughts and experience in your journal.

Walk or drive out into the country to a lonely place, ideally on an overcast day or at dusk so that you may experience the gloom and darkness of the day and moment of Jesus' death. Take with you a pad and some chalk or pencils.

Find a place to sit down. Simply be silent and let the loneliness enter into your heart. We have all known moments when we have felt abandoned or disappointed by friends. Think of one of these moments and stay in the silence with Jesus and his cry from the cross: 'My God, my God, why have you forsaken me?'

Draw a bleak landscape and a barren hill; put three crosses on the hill. Name the picture.

After at least 10 or 15 minutes of silent reflection, write a prayer sharing with Jesus your thoughts and feelings.

# The resurrection of Jesus

## Easter Day

Read Matthew 28:1–10.

One way to prayerfully approach a scripture text is the practice of *lectio divina* (Latin for 'sacred reading'): a prayerful and meditative reading of the text.

One way of doing this is:

- Go through the text and find some of the key words (use www.biblegateway.com).
- Who are the characters? Describe them.
- What is happening?
- What message is given for the early Christians?
- Meditate on the text for its spiritual content.
- What message does it have for you?
- Write a short prayer.

Use this method with Matthew 28:1–15.

The first day of the week after the Jewish sabbath, the two Marys come to the tomb. They do not know that Jesus has risen. The first day of the week becomes the Christian Sunday and replaces the sabbath. Sunday is a weekly day to celebrate the resurrection. A great event has happened, accompanied by signs and wonders, an earthquake and the presence of God's messenger to roll back the stone.

The text describes the appearance of the angel as like lightning and his clothing white as snow, an indication of his heavenly origin. He shone with the glory of God. The two Marys and the guards were witnesses to these events, but respond in vastly different ways. The text says the guards were filled with fear and became like dead men because they saw the angel and the stone rolled back. Their hearts were not touched by this great event and they allowed themselves to be bribed to say Jesus' body had been taken away.

The angel spoke to the women: 'Do not be afraid.' Jesus had been raised, and the angel commissioned them to go to Galilee and announce the good news to the disciples. They were filled with awe, a holy fear of the wonderful thing that had happened, and also with 'great joy' (v. 8, NRSV). Unlike the guards, they believed and were filled with wonder at God's goodness. They ran in their eagerness to tell the good news and on their way met Jesus. They fall at his feet and worship. Jesus repeats the angel's words: 'Do not be afraid; go and tell my brothers to go to Galilee; there they will see me' (v. 10).

Belief in the resurrection is the foundation of our Christian faith, but so often, it is not convenient to believe in Jesus, not economically or politically safe. Like the guards we can shut our minds and hearts to the signs of God's presence in our lives. If we would dare to risk following Jesus and searching for his presence in the great and small events of our day, we would hear Jesus say, 'Do not be afraid. I am with you always.'

# Birds of a feather

*Lynne Chitty*

## Consider the birds

### Introduction

Jesus was preaching in the open air when he invited his hearers to consider the birds (Matthew 6:26). They wouldn't have had to look far. Birds would have been their companions, as they are ours nearly everywhere we go today. There are over 9000 species. The tiniest is the bee humming bird which weighs 0.056 ounces. The heaviest is the ostrich which can weigh up to 30 stone! John Stott coined the term 'orni-theology' in his book *The Birds Our Teachers* and invites us, as Jesus did, to reflect on these amazingly diverse and resourceful creatures.

I invite you too to consider the birds, starting with a poem by Elizabeth Jennings called 'The Sparrows' Chorus', which is well worth looking up. In it the sparrows at first bemoan their ordinariness and their drab colours, but then puff themselves up and extol their qualities: their gratitude at the crumbs we share, their faithfulness in staying with us all through winter. In fact, they are little feathered miracles; they survive the harsh climate and their smallness is their gift.

What bird do you most feel like? What bird would you most like to be? You might like to draw or paint your answers. If you get a chance, feed some birds near you and spend time listening to their song of life.

# Slowly, slowly

## Going out

One of my favourite jobs is looking after the chickens and collecting the eggs. While they might not come out wrapped in chocolate like the ones I enjoy most, it is a wonderful moment to hold a freshly laid, still-warm egg in your hand.

A nun from Ghana once shared a proverb with me:

*Kakra kakra akoko benum nsno—*
Slowly, slowly, the hen drinks water.

That has stayed with me, especially when I watch our hens drink and they lift their beaks towards the sky. It offers an opportunity to look at our lives, which are so much about achieving and busyness, and to think about stillness and space and peace when the world seems to be the complete opposite, full of rush and noise. Some days, even when you first get up, there's an overwhelming sense that there is too much to do and you are tired before you even start. Living in a retreat house is no different; we are blessed with a wonderful setting, and opportunities to find space and silence, but there are still many practical things to do which can eat away at peace of mind and threaten the sense of God's presence that we try to rest in and enjoy.

Stilling the space within ourselves, drinking slowly, doesn't just happen; it comes from deep longing, deep thirst, even sometimes deep pain. So how can we nurture, protect and rejoice in a sense of stillness within? What does it mean to be still? It isn't about sitting idly doing nothing, but it's savouring the moment. It's being blessed with a sense of our place in the world, of being safe in the hands of the creator God who made us, of being connected with the mystery of life.

So if you get an opportunity, collect eggs or watch a bird in the garden drink, or even drink a glass of water yourself, drinking slowly, feeling it going down your throat, deep into you. What might you learn about being still, about finding a moment of calm in the midst of a hectic day, of appreciating a simple thing like water? Think about the mystery of life, the joy of life. Not cheap joy, but the joy that had first to endure the cross; the joy of risen life, the joy of hope.

## Disclosure

### Poetry/creative

*Prayer is like waiting for the kingfisher.*
*All you can do is*
*Be where he is likely to appear and*
*Wait.*
*Often, nothing much happens;*
*There is space, silence and expectancy.*
*No visible sign, only the knowledge*
*That he's been there,*
*And may come again.*
*Seeing or not seeing cease to matter,*
*You have been prepared.*
*But sometimes, when you've almost*
*Stopped expecting it,*
*A flash of brightness*
*Gives encouragement!*

Ann Lewin, *Watching for the Kingfisher*, Inspire, 2004 (used with permission)

Open-ended waiting is disturbing to those who like to be in control, and even people of faith struggle with the 'not knowing' that accompanies a period of waiting upon God. Yet we are invited to embrace the unpredictable nature of God's disclosure, not least in prayer. The ability to wait is a mark of maturity, revealing both patience, a fruit of the Spirit, and desire, the source of our longing. If prayer is like waiting for the kingfisher, then all you can do is be where he is likely to be and wait quietly.

How often does prayer seem uneventful—there's nothing to show for it? And yet, like the birdwatcher, we can't resist offering our time and attention again and again because we *know* God is there, just like the kingfisher.

There is space, silence and expectancy in prayer. When we make space for God in the busyness of our everyday lives, we give priority to what we value. Clearing our diary (or at least a portion of it) must be matched by a clearing of our mind so that the distractions that so often come along can be set aside. At the root of the word 'salvation' is the notion of space—God brings us to a spacious place and we in turn respond by offering him space to speak and influence us.

As for silence—it is *sometimes* the absence of speech, but always the act of listening. Indeed, 'listen' is an anagram of 'silent'. Silence is a chance to let go of words so the Word can come, God's living Word. Our God is a God of surprises who, like the kingfisher, is not at our beck and call. Responsive but not tame!

A flash of blue, a glimpse, a sense of the presence and the otherness of God can transform our prayer time and our lives.

Create a picture using any medium or material and add a flash of blue to it. Display it where you have your quiet time and let it encourage you to wait expectantly.

Or go outside and practise waiting, and be ready to be surprised by what you see or hear.

# A simple liturgy

## Prayer

*Ubi aves, ibi angeli—*
Where there are birds there are angels.
Thomas Aquinas

*A wise old owl lived in an oak.*
*The more he heard, the less he spoke.*
*The less he spoke, the more he heard.*
*Why aren't we all like that old bird?*
Proverb

***The light of the world is here among us, so we rejoice that we are not alone.***
***As a new day breaks and the song of the birds heralds the dawn, may new hope and courage sing in our hearts.***

***Blessed be this day... and all it will bring.***
***Blessed be this place... and all who are here.***
***Blessed be this time... and all time. Amen***

Spend a few moments praying for the peace of the world, for the enrichment of all creation and for all those you know who are struggling.

Get up early to listen to the dawn chorus or look on the internet for a recording.

***May the song of the birds be our music,***
***The flight of the birds inspire our freedom,***
***And may God, Father, Son and Holy Spirit, bless us today and every day. Amen***

# The runner duck

## Going out

*Three times*
*I looked up*
*as I struggled for words to finish my piece on prayer.*

*Three times*
*Runner Duck peered back through the glass of my cabin*
*'Look at me!'*

*As I watched him preen and peck*
*and settle down to a vigil of doing nothing*
*the prayer came*
*and I smiled as I finished my work and went to say*
*thank you.*

*But the duck*
*had gone off in search of more interesting company*
*and more forthcoming food.*

Taking time out to walk or bird watch need not just be for pleasure; it can be a necessity—a release of all the pressures that can easily build up inside us. It is when we feel we have the least time or when our 'to do' list is at its longest that the need to stop is at its greatest. That's often when the computer needs to be switched off or the stack of ironing put away and our walking boots and coats need to be got out.

It is when we stop searching for answers that they come; when we stop trying to solve all our problems at once that solutions gradually form; when we can't pray that suddenly we find we have been praying.

However busy you are today, make a conscious effort to let go of the demands of those things uppermost on your mind. Go for a walk, or watch the birds through your window. Look at pictures in a book of places that you would like to go to, or get out photographs of places you have enjoyed. Afterwards, make yourself a drink and a treat and cherish yourself. Allow God to reach through your concerns and your anxieties. Consider the birds, consider yourself and know that your heavenly Father loves you.

## Migration and faithfulness

### Imaginative

Three amazing bird facts and a beautifully haunting poem by R.S. Thomas called 'Migration' end our reflections on birds.

Every year the Arctic tern undertakes an epic journey to mate. After sojourning in the Antarctic, it heads off to the other end of the globe to breed in the Arctic—a return journey of more than 22,000 miles each year. The bird weighs only 4 ounces!

The royal albatross can live more than 60 years, but is very young and immature when it begins courting. The courtship is tender but polite, lasting four years. Once the birds have chosen each other, they will never choose again. However, life dictates that they cannot always be together. Sometimes they have to separate for a whole year, but they always come back to the same craggy rock where they first met to mate again. Their bond is unbreakable throughout their long lives and, no matter where they travel, they will always find each other.

A European swift can travel 500 miles a day and over a lifetime covers about 3 million miles.

Thomas' poem is about absence and presence, of knowing amidst unknowing, trusting the needle of our spirit to take us north where even in the bleakness the light of God can permeate the darkness.

Light a candle, and if you have a compass, place it beside you. Otherwise, draw one. Imagine yourself as a bird flying north, following the call of your heart. Flying over deserts, over ice and seas. Unsure and yet certain of where you are heading.

When you are ready, close with this prayer:

*Lord, as a bird stretches out its wings and soars higher and higher, held by the currents of your spirit, clear of the certainty of the ground, and trusting the eternal instinct of grace, so may my life awaken to the call of freedom and be released from all that would keep it earthbound. Draw me deeper into yourself, I pray. Amen*

# As a Child

*Phil Steer*

## Called

> ***Jesus* called *the children to him...***
> LUKE 18:16, NIV 1984, emphasis mine

Jesus was forever calling out to people. He called children to come to him. He called crowds to listen and understand his message (Mark 7:14). He called the sick to be healed (Matthew 20:32–34; Luke 13:12–13), and the dead to be raised to life (John 11:43). He called four fishermen to follow him, promising to make them 'fishers of men' (Matthew 4:18–22). He called twelve apostles, giving them power and authority to drive out demons and to cure diseases, and sending them out to preach the kingdom of God and to heal the sick (Luke 9:1–2). He called all kinds of people in order that he might transform their lives and so empower them to transform the lives of others.

Perhaps in part because of this we tend to attach a great deal of importance to the whole concept of 'calling'. We are encouraged to 'consider our calling' and to 'discover God's plan' for our lives. Countless books have been written on the subject and countless sermons preached. There are courses and conferences, studies and seminars. There are even personality tests that promise to provide an insight into our character and gifting, and hence some indication of our calling. We talk about it and we pray about it. We ask ourselves, 'Just what does God have in store for me? What does he want me to do?'

This concern with our calling arises from the very best of intentions: from a desire to identify the ways in which God might wish to use us, and in which we might best use our gifts and abilities to further his kingdom; to help us to see that we each have a unique part to play; to encourage and challenge us to step out in faith and make a difference in the world.

Unfortunately the effect of such introspection can be the very opposite of what is intended. Far from helping and encouraging us, it can instead leave us feeling frustrated and disappointed: frustrated that we don't seem able to hear God's call on our lives, and disappointed as we conclude that perhaps this means he has no particular use for us.

It might be all very well for those who have a strong sense of calling, such as those whose job is also their vocation (a word rooted in the Latin for 'voice', and so literally meaning 'what the voice called you to do'). But many others—myself included—feel no such call. We are where we are and do what we do, not because we have responded to some specific calling, but simply because... well, just because.

For example, at present I work in the City of London for a Lloyd's underwriting agent (yes, you might well ask!). My position there is not, I can assure you, something that I ever aimed to achieve or planned to do. It just happens to be where I've ended up, something that I've found my way into. It is a role that makes use of my abilities, experience and knowledge. I find it challenging and satisfying (although not, of course, all of the time). And, for me most importantly of all, it provides the income to support my family. It is, in a word, my job. I trust that God is with me in it and uses me through it, but in no way would I consider it to be a calling or vocation.

Indeed, to be quite truthful, I really don't have specific goals in life that I strive to achieve. My approach has always been more to take opportunities as they arise rather than to make opportunities happen. My epitaph might read, 'Let's just see how things pan out'! I'm not sure that this is necessarily any better or worse than a more directed approach; it is just different. Some sense a clear calling and vision and some don't—that's just how it is.

But such a specific sense of calling is just one facet of the far greater and wider-ranging call that God makes to us and upon our lives. And we can see this perhaps most clearly in Jesus' calling of children.

For when Jesus called the children, he did so not in order to give them some specific task or role. He did not call them to do anything or to be anything, but simply to be with him. 'Let the little children come to me' (Matthew 19:14). And the children came, not because they hoped to hear his plan for their lives or be envisioned and empowered to fulfil his purposes, but simply because they were attracted by his life and by his love, and they wanted to be around him.

This too is our primary calling: to come to Jesus and to be with him—not in some complex, mystical, spiritual sense, and not for any particular purpose, but simply as a little child would come to her father or mother or sister or brother; for no other reason than that this is family, this is where she belongs, and that she wants to be with them.

In his account of the early Church, Luke records that 'when they [the rulers and elders and teachers of the law] saw the courage of Peter and John and realised that they were unschooled, ordinary men, they were astonished and they took note that these men had been with Jesus' (Acts 4:13). For all that the apostles went on to achieve for the kingdom of God, it began with this simple yet fundamental fact: they had been with Jesus. This is the call that comes before all others, upon which all other calls are founded, and from which all other callings flow.

Secondly, Jesus called the children simply to be themselves: 'He called a little child and had him stand among them' (Matthew 18:2). Jesus called this little child to proclaim the truth and reality of the kingdom of God, not only to the crowd gathered on that day, but to all who would hear and read and receive this gospel account throughout all the years that would follow. Quite a calling. Yet the little child did not have to say or do anything special; indeed, he did not have to say or do anything at all. He simply had to stand among the crowd and be himself, be the person that God had created, be a little child.

In the same way, before God calls us to do anything particular, he calls us simply to stand as a witness to the people amongst whom we find ourselves; to stand as the person that he has created us to be, as the person that he is recreating in Christ, as a person who is receiving and revealing the kingdom of God as a little child.

None of which is to suggest that God does not call individuals (and groups) to fulfil particular tasks or take on particular roles—of course he does. The Bible is full of such stories, as is the history of the Church down through the ages, and God continues to call his people to serve him in specific ways, both 'great' and 'small'. Neither is it to say that God might not call you or me in such a way, nor that we need not be attentive and responsive to any such call—of course he might and of course we must. Indeed, even I, for all my lack of vision, have had times where I have felt, 'This is where God wants me to be right now, this is what he wants me to do.'

Yet if we become preoccupied with the task of trying to 'discover our calling', then we run the risk of missing all that God has already called us to be. He has called us to belong to Jesus (Romans 1:6), to be in fellowship with him (1 Corinthians 1:9), and to be transformed into his likeness (Romans 8:28–30). He has called us to be holy (2 Timothy 1:9), to endure suffering

(1 Peter 2:21), to be a blessing to others (1 Peter 3:9), and to be a people of peace (Colossians 3:15). He has called us to freedom (Galatians 5:13), and to hope (Ephesians 1:18), and to life eternal (1 Timothy 6:12). He has called us heavenward (Philippians 3:14), out of darkness into light (1 Peter 2:9), that we might share in Christ's glory (2 Thessalonians 2:14).

What a calling this is! If we could but truly hear it and receive it and respond to it, what a difference it would make, both to ourselves and to all who would then see the reality of God's kingdom revealed in us. This is our ultimate calling: to come to Jesus as little children, to receive his kingdom as little children and to live our lives as true children of our heavenly Father.

# Spotlight: Stepping into quiet spaces at Holy Rood House

*Elizabeth Baxter*

Step across the threshold with me as I open the gate to Holy Rood House, nestling beneath the hills in North Yorkshire. Holy Rood House, Centre for Health and Pastoral Care in Thirsk, opened its doors in 1993 as an Ecumenical Healing Retreat and Theology Centre. The charity began in the 1970s at Spennithorne Home of Healing near Leyburn as a response to the Churches' Ministry of Healing. The charity works closely with the medical services, charitable agencies, educational institutions and churches and is in partnership with The Guild of Health and St Raphael.

> I felt lonely but from the time I came through those gates
> I felt at peace...

This is one of several quotes included in this article, written by guests in the small books in the bedrooms.

Tall pines beckon us as we leave behind the bustling market town of Thirsk, entering a gentle, creative space, an oasis for guests at a time of need. Here we discover safer space at times when life feels unsafe. Spotting the first snowdrops, we walk to the porch, finding a warm, spontaneous welcome.

> *Thank you for the peace in my heart*
> *For the feeling of closeness to God*

*For the stability and security*
*That Holy Rood brings*
*To all who enter through the door.*

This Edwardian house, previously Holy Rood Convent, is infused with the prayer of the Sisters, who left in 1992, and the hope and vision of the present community. My husband Stanley and I have been here for 22 years since the charity opened the doors to those seeking healing and acceptance. Come with me as we meet those who work here, counsellors, masseurs, chaplains, gardeners, those providing hospitality and many others who make Holy Rood a special place.

> I loved the simplicity of Holy Rood House. The discovery—gradual discovery—of all the nooks and crannies and thoughtfulness of the personal touches—flowers, books, pictures... a healing and very calming place for me.

Through our holistic approach we seek to embody the hope of the Christian story, making connections with individual and community stories. Therapeutic and theological aspects of our ministry inform each other.

> For someone who struggles with the institutional church, this is a haven, a space to be, a safe place, a place to journey inwardly.

Flowers in every room bring life to those who feel lost and worn down, as so many people say, 'I don't know who I am any more.' God's loving presence becomes tangible through little things, and this is healing for all of us at Holy Rood.

> I discovered the awesome power of inactivity to unlock our deepest recesses and the power of God to heal through imaginative processes. This week I rediscovered myself and discovered for the first time parts of myself...

Here are different kinds of spaces, where we can relax with others, and then more contained, quiet spaces. Walking to the chapel, we become aware of the journey of healing, moving from the shared, inclusive table in the dining room to the altar. At both tables we break bread together, sustaining us, as part of the gentle spirituality undergirding our daily rhythm of community life, engaging the senses through the sacraments and healing prayer.

> I have been reminded here that I do not travel alone; that others are Christ to me and I to them. We are all broken, all needing healing—there is no shame, and there needs be no loneliness.

There is a map of the world to prevent us from becoming insular as we hold prayers for justice and peace. Embodiment finds an integral place in our healing processes, so stop a while with me, be still, and sense the quiet presence of God before we make our way into the gardens.

> I look around at the pictures, the garden, the chapel, the sculptures and sense these glorious aspects of Holy Rood are the rainbows its light has created through the veil of tears it has witnessed.
>
> What a privilege it has been to reach out and touch that rainbow.

I think you will see how Holy Rood weaves the quiet space of the chapel with the labyrinth and hidden places of the gardens, echoing other quiet spaces where someone listens quietly to another, accompanying them through a difficult journey.

*I came unable to find peace within myself*
*I leave with the stirrings of stillness gradually dawning*
*I needed love*
*you loved me*
*I needed to be held*
*you held me*
*I needed to be surrounded by warmth, softness and gentleness*
*you enfolded me*
*I was frightened*
*your calm strength gave me some peace.*

Can you hear the birds greet us and have you noticed how the goats (Phoebe, Freya and Meg) offer us unconditional acceptance? Let's stop a while in the pond garden, surrounded by fruits and herbs. We make connections with the harvest of our own lives, as all is harvested and used in the meals we enjoy. Watching the water lily and the ducklings moves me to prayers of thanksgiving for this holy space where poems have been written, decisions made and tears shed.

I came to Holy Rood House not knowing what to expect, uncertain of what I would find. I found beautiful gardens of herbs and flowers, with gorgeous scents when touched, a quiet peaceful atmosphere...

Let's peep into the hidden garden and Chapel of Sophia. Sophia, Greek for Wisdom, is important to the community as we work alongside so many people at a crossroads in their lives (see

Proverbs 8 and 9). Here, away from everyone, we can go to those places deep within us, without fear, knowing we are held tenderly. I am grateful for the presence of Sophia accompanying us through difficult times, awakening our own possibilities of healing. Wounded we may be, yet together in these quiet spaces we are able to support each other and find ourselves beloved.

*The spirit is freedom,*
*She is movement*
*She is process*
*She is wisdom*
*She is breath—she blew me here.*

Creative arts take place in Thorpe House, next door. You may be pleasantly surprised by this imposing, yet most welcoming house, with conference rooms, gallery and library. Step this way and you will find the art room, vibrant and liberating. Our art therapist provides safe space for us to work through creative processes at a deep level.

I was at the edge—Holy Rood House gave me time and safe space to step back from the edge.

Therapy is followed by a good night's sleep at Holy Rood when we close the curtains on the world and nestle in to our own space, prepared for us with love and care.

I came in despair and anguish and utter pain.
You held my story and placed me in a room of Peace, offering me sanctuary and space to begin to find the healing I needed... I discovered a gentle God, love and acceptance.

One of our first guests wrote the poem below, and my prayer is that we may always be a place of hope. Your presence with me helps to make this possible. Thank you for sharing this journey, which will have an effect on us both and enrich the healing ministry of Holy Rood House.

*I came to this house*
*wearing my dark cloak—*
*of powerlessness—*
*laid it on the ground*
*for all to see.*
*Friends picked it up—*
*circling the hem*
*they danced with it*
*tossed it skyward*
*like a parachute game—*
*to reveal small shoots*
*of power and hope*
*growing under wraps.*

---

The Revd Elizabeth Baxter is Executive Director of Holy Rood House and enjoys accompanying people on their therapeutic and theological journeys. For more information, see www.holyroodhouse.org.uk.

# BRF Quiet Days

BRF Quiet Days are an ideal way of redressing the balance in our busy lives. Held in peaceful locations around the country, each one is led by an experienced speaker and gives the opportunity to reflect, be silent and pray, and, through it all, to draw closer to God.

Here is part of the programme for 2017:

Tuesday 7 March: 'The Living Cross' led by Amy Boucher Pye at St Paul's Church, 50 Long Lane, Finchley, London N3 2PU

Thursday 1 June: 'Finding God in a Garden' led by Jennifer Rees Larcombe at The House of Retreat, The Street, Pleshey, Chelmsford CM3 1HA

Thursday 9 November: 'Marks upon the Heart: pilgrim journeys, lessons for life' led by Sally Welch at The Carmelite Priory, Boars Hill, Oxford OX1 5HB

For further details and to book, and for information about other Quiet Days in 2017, please go to **brfonline.org.uk/events-and-quiet-days** or contact us at BRF, 15 The Chambers, Vineyard, Abingdon OX14 3FE; tel: +44 (0)1865 319700.

Finding God in all things, hearing God's voice for ourselves and others… the *Quiet Spaces Prayer Journal* will help you to develop and maintain a life of creative prayer. With space to write, quotations drawn from Christian tradition and from *Quiet Spaces* to aid reflection, this is ideal for you or as a gift for anyone wanting to deepen their prayer life.

# QUIET SPACES SUBSCRIPTION FORM

All our Bible reading notes can be ordered online by visiting
**biblereadingnotes.org.uk/subscriptions**

If you and a minimum of **four** friends subscribe to *Quiet Spaces* or BRF's other Bible reading notes (*New Daylight*, *Day by Day with God*, *Guidelines*, *The Upper Room*), you can form a group. What's so good about being in a group? You pay the price of the notes only —postage is free for delivery to a UK address. (All notes are sent to one address.) All group orders are invoiced. No advance payment is required. For more information, see **biblereadingnotes.org.uk/group-subscriptions** or contact the BRF office.

Title ........... First name/initials ............. Surname ...................................

Address ..................................................................................

.............................................................. Postcode ......................

Telephone ......................... Email ...................................................

**INDIVIDUAL SUBSCRIPTION** Please send *Quiet Spaces* beginning with the May 2017 / September 2017 / January 2018 issue (*delete as appropriate*):

| | Quantity | UK | Europe | Rest of world |
|---|---|---|---|---|
| (per 3 issues) | ☐ | ☐ £16.40 | ☐ £24.60 | ☐ £28.50 |

Total enclosed £ ................ (cheques should be made payable to 'BRF')

Please charge my MasterCard / Visa ☐ Debit card ☐ with £ ................

Card no. ☐☐☐☐ ☐☐☐☐ ☐☐☐☐ ☐☐☐☐

Valid from M M Y Y Expires M M Y Y Security code* ☐☐☐

Last 3 digits on the reverse of the card

Signature* ................................................ Date ...... /...... /......

*ESSENTIAL IN ORDER TO PROCESS YOUR ORDER

To set up a Direct Debit, please also complete the Direct Debit instruction on the reverse of this form.

**GROUP SUBSCRIPTION (UK only)** Please send *Quiet Spaces* beginning with the May 2017 / September 2017 / January 2018 issue (*delete as appropriate*):

Quantity ☐ (Current price per issue: £4.40)

Please invoice me: per issue / annually (*delete as appropriate*).

**Please return this form to:**

BRF, 15 The Chambers, Vineyard, Abingdon OX14 3FE

To read our terms and find out about cancelling your order, please visit **brfonline.org.uk/terms**.



**QS0117**

The Bible Reading Fellowship

# Instruction to your bank or building society to pay by Direct Debit

Please fill in the whole form using a ballpoint pen and return it to:
BRF, 15 The Chambers, Vineyard, Abingdon OX14 3FE

Service User Number: | 5 | 5 | 8 | 2 | 2 | 9 |

Name and full postal address of your bank or building society

| To: The Manager | Bank/Building Society |
|---|---|
| Address | |
| | |
| | |
| | Postcode |

Name(s) of account holder(s)

| |
|---|
| |

Branch sort code

| | | – | | | – | | |
|---|---|---|---|---|---|---|---|

Bank/Building Society account number

| | | | | | | | |
|---|---|---|---|---|---|---|---|

Reference number

| | | | | | | |
|---|---|---|---|---|---|---|

Instruction to your Bank/Building Society
Please pay The Bible Reading Fellowship Direct Debits from the account detailed in this instruction, subject to the safeguards assured by the Direct Debit Guarantee. I understand that this instruction may remain with The Bible Reading Fellowship and, if so, details will be passed electronically to my bank/building society.

| Signature(s) |
|---|
| |

Banks and Building Societies may not accept Direct Debit instructions for some types of account.

## DIRECT DEBIT PAYMENT

You can pay for your annual subscription to our Bible reading notes using Direct Debit. You need only give your bank details once, and the payment is made automatically every year until you cancel it. If you would like to pay by Direct Debit, please use the form opposite, entering your BRF account number under 'Reference number'.

You are fully covered by the Direct Debit Guarantee:

### The Direct Debit Guarantee

- This Guarantee is offered by all banks and building societies that accept instructions to pay Direct Debits.
- If there are any changes to the amount, date or frequency of your Direct Debit, The Bible Reading Fellowship will notify you 10 working days in advance of your account being debited or as otherwise agreed. If you request The Bible Reading Fellowship to collect a payment, confirmation of the amount and date will be given to you at the time of the request.
- If an error is made in the payment of your Direct Debit, by The Bible Reading Fellowship or your bank or building society, you are entitled to a full and immediate refund of the amount paid from your bank or building society.
- If you receive a refund you are not entitled to, you must pay it back when The Bible Reading Fellowship asks you to.
- You can cancel a Direct Debit at any time by simply contacting your bank or building society. Written confirmation may be required. Please also notify us.

This page is for your notes.